# Savvy Senior Sabbaticals

For Carolina –
May you be encouraged by
this Savvy Senior Sabbatical book!
Samantha
9/15/20

# Savvy Senior Sabbaticals

by Samantha Landy

Desert Ministries
La Quinta, CA

The devotionals in this book are based on newspaper columns by Samantha Landy, The Way...As I See It.

Savvy Senior Sabbaticals


Editor, Georgeann De Woody
Published by Desert Ministries
La Quinta, CA

Library of Congress Control Number: 2005907753
Library of Congress Cataloging-in-Publications Data

Cover Design: Angie Druetta and Georgeann DeWoody

Landy, Samantha
Savvy Senior Sabbaticals/Samantha Landy

ISBN 0-9715184-8-3
1. Devotionals-Christianity



*Samantha Landy Ministries*

PO Box 911701

St. George, UT 84791

www.SamanthaLandy.com

# *Dedication*

To all of my friends around the world,
Senior and not so Senior,
who have enriched my life.
And most of all, to my Lord and Savior,
who will abundantly give wisdom
to all of us on this stage
of our journey as Savvy Seniors.

# Table of Contents


Introduction........................................ xi

Listen to Your Broccoli........................................ 1

Forgetful Forays........................................ 3

Be A Miracle........................................ 6

Uninhibited Joy........................................ 8

Choose Life........................................ 11

If Only........................................ 13

Enjoy Life........................................ 15

Whatever He Says........................................ 17

Bless Israel........................................ 20

Roll With the Punches........................................ 23

The Auction........................................ 26

The Pie Social........................................ 29

God Bless America........................................ 31

Self Perceptions........................................ 34

Grace and Joy........................................ 36

Restoration and Refuge........................................ 39

Trash Cans........................................ 42

Learn to Soar........................................ 45

His Creation........................................ 48

Heavenly Fruit Vendor........................................ 51

Unexplainable Predicaments........................................ 53

Do We Pendulate?........................................ 55

Your Shadow........................................ 57
A Seed in the Rock........................................ 59
Failure is Not Fatal........................................ 62
Delays Are Not Deadly........................................ 64
Pressures Are Not Permanent........................................ 66
Our Journey........................................ 68
Wisdom and Balance........................................ 70
Our DNA........................................ 72
Uniquely Loved........................................ 74
The Wisdom of Man........................................ 76
A Senior Moment........................................ 78
Mi Casa, Su Casa........................................ 80
Ideas, Concepts & Insights........................................ 82
Holiday Hassles........................................ 85
Walking in Wisdom........................................ 87
A Paradigm Shift........................................ 90
Divine Destiny........................................ 92
God's Timing........................................ 94
Great Hindsight........................................ 96
Crushed for You........................................ 99

# Introduction

As a Christian, it's always amazing to me when God Almighty intervenes in our lives in herculean, magnificent ways and alters the course of our lives forever. But then, it's just as incredible when He, Jehovah, the Most High God, chooses to speak to our hearts and answer those simple everyday needs we have.

Take for instance, a few days ago, my part time secretary, Stacey was helping me with the book orders for the "Savvy Singles Handbook," and in processing the paper work, we misplaced a check. It was a check for 12 books so it certainly wasn't one I wanted to forget about.

Later that night I had the idea to look out in the garbage. We had emptied all of the waste baskets from the office as the garbage man was coming in the morning. So I looked through all of the bags and couldn't find it. I looked again in the office and of course was praying, Lord, please help me find it. I really didn't want to call the person and tell them we had lost their check.

I had this sudden thought, go look in the garbage again. Logically, it didn't make any sense as I had been very thorough and it just wasn't there. But not finding it anywhere else, I figured I might as well look again, because in the early morning the men were coming to haul it away and it was now or never.

This time I looked inside every envelope whether it was the one belonging to the missing check or not. And in the very last bag, in the bottom of the large garbage container, there was the check, inside an envelope! How grateful I was for the prompting in my heart. How I rejoiced at His care, thankful I had followed the nudging of the Lord, even if it wasn't logical. Like you, I've discovered that many things in my walk with the Lord aren't necessarily logical. But many of the great Bible stories, if we look at them with our natural senses, aren't logical either. We have to look at them with the eyes of faith in order to understand them.

The same gentle nudging of the Lord happened this afternoon as I was driving down the road to take care of errands. As usual, I had my favorite Christian radio station on and was singing praise songs along with the radio. And in between, I was praying.

"What I really need, Lord, is a sabbatical. I'm so overworked and stressed. Yes, I'd like a sabbatical." As another song came on, I thought, where in the world did that come from? I don't normally use the word "sabbatical" in my prayers.

Just as quickly, the title, "Savvy Senior Sabbaticals," came into my mind. Wow! I had the title for this new devotional book! That's what we Seniors all need, is to get away from our over stressed and over processed lives, to a few moments of respite, a few moments to decompress and have some quiet time with our Lord.

Just to be sure I had the concept of the sabbatical correct; I went to my dog-eared dictionary. One of the definitions for sabbatical is, "any extended period of leave from one's customary work." Reading a devotional may not be considered an "extended period" but we all know, that when the presence of the Lord comes, even a few moments in time, can refresh us as though we had hours, days or weeks at rest.

So, read on "Savvy Senior" enjoy your sabbatical!

*Samantha*

# Listen to Your Broccoli!

Rereading the book, "Bird by Bird," Annie Lamont the author, says, "To be a good writer, you not only have to write a great deal but you have to care." She goes on to say that as a writer, she thinks we should try to be part of the solution, try to understand a little about life, to have hope and to pass that on.

And then she goes even further and says each human being needs to learn to "listen to your broccoli." For some weird reason only she fully understands, she calls her inner self, her intuition, her broccoli. Some people say women have a more fully developed intuition than men and perhaps that is so. There have been times in my life when deep down in my belly, or my broccoli, if you prefer, I knew something wasn't right and when I have ignored it, it has often resulted in disaster.

I'm not a person who lives in the past or dwells on the past. If there is a situation I can't do anything about, I have learned just to pray about it and let it go. It isn't always easy, but necessary. So last week, some friends I had not seen in some time, asked me what I had learned from certain events of my past. I was taken by surprise. But out of my belly, out of my broccoli, came this thought and I knew it was true. "Well, I have learned not to be so trusting."

Yet, as I said it, it made me a little sad. I like trusting people. I've enjoyed taking people at face value and believing if they said it, they would follow through. Have I lived a rather sheltered life in the past? Perhaps. Have I looked at life with rose-colored glasses? I hope so. I would always rather be an optimist than a pessimist. No, sir, that half-empty glass is not for me!

Nevertheless, I understand that even as I write, the next 24 hours might be the most difficult of our lives. What will this year really be like for us? We may not be able to control our circumstances, often our predicaments reflect other people's decisions whether we like it or not. So, what to do?

One of the best ways to transform our lives is to change our attitude about our life. I remember reading some time ago a statement from Chuck Swindoll about attitude. He said that "Attitude is more important than education. Attitude is more important than money. Attitude is more important than background. It is everything!"

Want to revolutionize your life? Change your attitude. Let me tell you something. I'm not exactly an expert, but at least a well traveled pilgrim on this journey called life. I can tell you this: Your life can begin to change in an instant. You can start your life over today and make this the best year you ever had!

How? First of all, simply ask Jesus Christ to come in to your life and forgive you of your sins. Sound complicated? No, it is just the opposite. It's so simple many people don't get it. You can even use the words I just wrote, it's that simple. But the real metamorphosis happens when you get a Bible and begin to read it, asking God to show you how to live a contented, fulfilled life. Then ask God to help you change your attitude. And He will.

King David knew the importance of attitude also, he said in *Psalm 39:7, "My hope is in You, Oh Lord."*

**Prayer:**

Dear Lord, thank You for bringing comfort and new direction to my life. I trust You to help me be contented and fulfilled. My hope is in You! Amen

# *Forgetful Forays*

The following story is about being forgetful. Sometimes we don't feel forgetting something is funny, but we can never laugh too much, especially at ourselves.

It seems two elderly ladies had been friends for many decades. Over the years, they had shared all kinds of activities and adventures. Lately, their activities had been limited to meeting a few times a week to play cards. One day, they were playing cards when one looked at the other and said, "Now don't get mad at me. I know we've been friends for a long time, but I just can't think of your name! I've thought and thought, but I can't remember it. Please tell me what your name is."

Her friend glared at her. For at least three minutes she just stared and glared at her. Finally she said, "How soon do you need to know?" (smile!)

Thankfully, I'm not that bad, but there are days........

I've been thinking about being forgetful and I've come to a conclusion. Now that we are in that over-fifty five age group, it just may be that we are too hard on ourselves.

Take for instance, when I lose my car keys; my grandson has done that too. Or I leave some important mail at home that I wanted to take to the post office; my twenty-four year old secretary has done that. Perhaps the take-out container is left on the restaurant table; dinner companions of all ages have done that. Wearing shoes that are similar but not a pair is not relegated to only me; my pastor who is in his forties told that story on himself. Wearing only one earring…some people even do that on purpose!

Get the picture? Maybe, just maybe if we would slow down our life a little, we might not be on such overload and the "forgetfulness" would dissipate. I know, I know some people reading this book are in that age they call retirement, but I'm amazed at how many people have told me that they are busier now than when they were working.

While being busy is a good thing if we handle it properly and enjoy our activities, if it causes us frustration, then it's not.

We've all met people (I hope you're not one of them) that are busy, but in that busyness, live in constant turmoil. They're always upset, always frustrated, always having some kind of challenge that keeps them from sleeping. So then they awaken tired and start the day all over again, frustrated and now tired too! You may want to order my CD, "Midnight Meditations" a CD full of old hymns and scripture to help you go to sleep.

Normally, it's not the big things in life that get us upset. For some reason, most of us rise to the occasion when we have something catastrophic to deal with. We manage to take a deep breath, pray, get a second opinion and look at our options.

But it's in the small irritations of life where we often lose it. Author Philip Yancey made a statement many years ago, which has since become a household mantra. It's "don't sweat the small stuff."

Why is it important not to get frustrated over the small stuff, like forgetting where we put something? Not only will it affect everyone in our world but we can ruin our own day too and shoot up our blood pressure as well.

God promises to give us peace, not as the world gives, peace on the inside of us. But it's up to us to tap into His peace. The way we do that is to choose to keep a good attitude, choose to be happy. If you're struggling with choosing to be happy and want to learn more about it, you could get a copy of my book, "Savvy Singles Handbook." (smile) Even if you're married, I think it would encourage you to be happy. That's God's best for you, married or single, young or old……forgetful or not!

**Prayer:**

Father God, I am grateful that while I may forget to spend time with You—I am always on Your mind. Through Kind David You reminded me that You never slumber or sleep but are thinking about me all the time. Father, help me slow down a little. If I am constantly on the run I may miss something special You have for me. I want to know You in a deeper way. Amen

**Personal Thoughts:**

____________________________________________

____________________________________________

____________________________________________

____________________________________________

____________________________________________

____________________________________________

____________________________________________

____________________________________________

# Be a Miracle

Albert Einstein is quoted as saying, "There are two ways to live your life. One, as though nothing is a miracle. The other, as though everything is a miracle."

All throughout our lives we have the choice of looking at life from either approach – nothing is a miracle or everything is a miracle.

The delight of my grandson, Shawn, upon seeing a little chipmunk; the beauty of pink and cream tiger lilies by the fence; my teenage granddaughter, Brandy, actually enjoying shopping with me; the last rays of the summer sun setting on the lake. Which will they be? A miracle or not?

Spokane, Washington has an exquisite golf course called The Creek at Qualchan Golf Course. My son, Randy and I love to play the course not only for the challenge of playing over creeks and hitting off of high cliffs but also for its beauty. Recently, I had the thrill of a perfectly hit chip shot, which ended up giving me a birdie on a par five. Now, that's definitely a miracle!

We have all read the dramatic stories of someone being rescued from a dangerous situation or a cancer lump disappearing with medicine or prayer. Those are biggies, definitely on the miracle side.

But what about the little events of life, those small nudges or the intuition we sense that turns our life around.

One such event happened some years ago to a friend of mine. Sandy had been invited to attend a writer's conference since she was writing her first book.

Knowing only one friend, she had much hesitation about going and almost did not attend. Yet, she had a nudge, a feeling she really should go.

While there, she had an opportunity to meet with one of the instructors, a well known author. He ended up becoming her husband. Had she not attended that conference they most likely would never have met since they lived in totally different areas of the United States. A miracle God planned?

Then there is the story of a woman on the breadline at the Franciscan Mission in New York City. She was asked if she was thankful for anything. “Sure,” she said. “I'm thankful I'm not dead and I'm thankful that yesterday I found a bottle of water in the garbage that nobody had drunk from. It was my very own new bottle of water.”

For those of us who have the opportunity to simply buy a bottle of water if we want it, that may not sound like much of a miracle. But for this lady, if you asked her, I imagine she would consider it a miracle...her very own new bottle of water.

Bradley James, a personal friend of Mother Teresa's tells of the many times Mother Teresa would give a sip of water to a dying man or woman on the streets of Calcutta. You might say, where was their miracle, they died. She would reply, “But they didn't die alone and unloved.” For me, that qualifies as a miracle. To think God would use a tiny lady from the convent, Mother Teresa, and she would find that one person in the mass of humanity, that one person who needed a sip of water and needed to know of God's love. That's a miracle.

Mother Teresa was fulfilling the scripture in John 7:37, where Jesus speaks and let's us know that it isn't just physical water, but also spiritual water that we need; she gave them both. There are many ways we can “be a miracle,” but it must start first of all in our head. Is everything a miracle or nothing a miracle? The choice is ours.

# Uninhibited Joy

It was a surprise birthday party to end all birthday parties. Even with time, the electric joy of the evening has not diminished.

As we talked about it afterwards, it was like a birthday party, the TV show "This is Your Life," and reality TV all rolled into one, only better; this was real.

My flight from California to Atlanta, Georgia to visit my friends had been scheduled long before the concept for Kathryn's birthday party even emerged, so I was happy to be there at the same time.

Weeks before the party, Gerald was having dinner with Charles and Kathryn, telling them about hearing this incredible singing group from New York. He had heard them at a Christian Conference in the mountains of South Carolina. A man named Brent organized the impressive group made up by various Broadway singers and musicians.

Listening to the conversation between Charles and Gerald, Kathryn tentatively asked, "Is his name Brent Sala, by any chance?"

"Well, I think so, yes, his last name was Sala." Gerald replied. At that, Kathryn's face became wreathed in smiles, "Oh, I can't believe it, I can't believe it! He was my very best friend in college and I have looked for him for 20 years, wondering where he was! I can't believe it might be him!" A phone call reunion was immediate.

Surprise plans were eventually made between Charles (Kathryn's husband) and Gerald for Kathryn's surprise birthday party to be held at Gerald's lovely home in Atlanta, flying in Brent as a surprise.

We worked all day preparing for the party. Gerald cooked and I was in charge of decorations. I tied helium balloons to the dining room chairs and hung streamers from the chandelier. I put out gold chargers for all ten place settings of white china with gold rimmed goblets and sterling place settings. We had five tall glass and brass candle holders in the middle of the table with fat, squatty candles.

On top of all this elegance, I piled the table high with toy horns, cameras, streamers, crayons for the coloring contest, glitter markers to assist the artist party goers, and piles of foil confetti so the taffeta table top was totally covered. With additional sprinkling of confetti on the white cloth napkins, the festive table was complete.

Soon Kathryn's parents and sister arrived from a neighboring city, another surprise for Kathryn when she was to arrive later. Brent had flown in earlier that day.

Kathryn was indeed surprised when she and Charles arrived, to see her family. Soon Gerald's cell phone rang. Gerald handed it to Kathryn saying, "Kathryn it's for you, it's Brent."

Even though they had talked numerous times since she had received the phone number from Gerald, she was thrilled Brent would call her on her birthday. The rest of us knew Brent was calling her from his cell phone standing only 20 feet away in the bedroom. As they talked, Brent said, "Do you remember a movie, when the actor called his friend from inside the house?" With that Kathryn looked up as Brent came out of the bedroom, still talking to her on the phone.

Kathryn laughed and screamed at the same time, running and hugging Brent as he scooped her up in his arms and swung her around and around like a little girl.

What joy! In the meantime, we were all snapping pictures of them at their 20-year reunion. It was a night none of us will ever forget.

I wonder if that was similar to the excitement and joy the father must have felt when his prodigal son returned, as Jesus described it in the Bible. I think it's also similar to the uninhibited joy our Father feels when one of us returns to Him, whether it is after a day or 20 years or a lifetime. *Luke* describes it in chapter *15:11-32. Verse 24 (AMP)* says, "...this my son was dead, and is alive again; he was lost, and is found! And they began to revel and feast and make merry."

**Prayer:**

Dear God, what a joy it must be to Your heart when one of Your children returns home to You. Thank You for loving and patiently waiting for me. Amen

**Personal Thoughts:**

______________________________________________

______________________________________________

______________________________________________

______________________________________________

______________________________________________

______________________________________________

______________________________________________

______________________________________________

______________________________________________

# Choose Life

Valentine's Day can be a tricky holiday or a warm fuzzy in our lives. One year it might be the Hallmark version with lovely cards, flowers and a romantic dinner. The next year it might be the loneliest holiday of the year, that is until we come to the next holiday and then we start all over.

The Valentine's Day after my husband, Morry died, I decided I wasn't going to ignore the day, but choose to live. So a few days before, I called up a friend whose husband had also died the previous year. She said she just planned to read a book and go to bed early and ignore the whole thing. I said, "Oh no, we're not! We are going to make a healthy choice. We are going out! It doesn't matter if the whole restaurant is full of couples."

After a little cajoling, I made reservations and on the appointed day Jennie and I went to one of my favorite restaurants where I knew the owner. Yes, it was full of couples but he gave us a lovely table and we were greeted warmly by the waiters.

While waiting for our salad, the owner brought over a carefully wrapped little box for each of us. In my box was a pewter key chain with a huge smiling sun on it. Looking at it just made me smile. Jennie's was similar.

After awhile he came back to our table to chat and of course I thanked him profusely for my Valentine's gift. Jennie ruefully said, "Thank you, it's the only gift I have received today."

He laughed and said, "Well, that's better than I did! I didn't get any!" And we all laughed together.

But it set me to thinking about our perspective in life. *Romans 8:6* says, *"...to be spiritually minded is life and peace."* As we begin to embrace the challenges of a new day, we need to open our mind and heart to God. As we do, quietly, the cares and concerns of our life, all of the seemingly impossible situations, will dissipate in their importance as we put God first. We need to know He cares for us and His agenda for us is always for good. Indeed, we can have a life of peace and joy if we remain spiritually minded.

When we have major life alterations such as divorce, death of a spouse or a catastrophic illness, life itself may be shouting for our attention. Yet, it is especially during these times, during the frantic race just to keep up with the myriad things that come at us, we need to stop and draw on the peace of God He offers us.

We need to remember to take a few moments sometime in our day to read a few scriptures and read a devotional that encourages us in our walk with the Lord. The simple act of talking to the Lord, taking a few moments to relax and quietly breathe in the Holy Spirit will bring us peace and joy in spite of our circumstances.

**Prayer:**

Heavenly Father, I trust You in the dark and lonely times to bring new life and the peace that is mine through Your Son, Jesus. And Father, through the Holy Spirit may I become an example to others of this new life and peace in You. Amen

# If Only...

The story of the man by the pool in Bethesda is written in *John 5:1-9.* Jesus was on his way to a feast in Jerusalem. As He walked by the pool where many sick and lame people lay, Jesus asked a man if he wanted to be made well. But the man said, *Verse 7 (LB) "Sir, if only I had a man to put me in the pool when the water is troubled, but while I am going another steps down before me."*

Without realizing it, many of us go through life with the phrase of "if only" on our lips and in our minds. That's what the sick man by the pool dwelt on too.

I met a man who told me years ago, he had a chance to buy (very cheaply) the oil leases on a large tract of land. He didn't and ten years later, that land became the Tioga Oil Tract. The largest oil bed in North Dakota. As he said, if only he had bought the leases, he could have been rich.

How often do we say, if only – maybe not such a dramatic thing as the oil leases, but it is an easy habit to get into to use for an excuse.

If only I had more time, I would read the Bible and pray and be a better person. If only I had the training as a child, I could have been a great painter or musician. If only I were taller, I could have been a star basketball player. If only I were better looking, I could have been a famous actor. If only I had a better education, I could have done so much more with my life. If we're not careful, we can defeat ourselves. Each of us can compile our own list of "if onlys."

Now, we don't know exactly how old the lame man was, he could easily have been like us, over 50 years old, for the Bible says that he had had his infirmity for thirty-eight years. He had been using his "if only" excuse for thirty-eight years! How long have we been doing it?

But just like us, Jesus wanted to come into his life and show him that he didn't need to hang on to his "if onlys" any longer! Jesus saw beyond his "if onlys" and saw the man's potential faith and said to him, *"Rise, take up your bed and walk."*

We too, could turn our "if only" around for a positive thing. "If only" we will look to Jesus for our strength and healing, we will find He is the power within us to overcome our feeble excuses for not developing our potential and God given talents, whatever our age.

Scientists have long affirmed we use a very small part of our brain capacity in our lifetime. So it would stand to reason even if we are in that age they call, Senior, we haven't used all of our brain potential. We really don't have to use that excuse, "if only," any more. Let's stand up and move toward those goals and dreams we have held so long. Indeed, Jesus is saying to us, *"Rise up, take up your bed and walk."* Rise up and let God help you walk into your God-given dreams and hearts desires.

**Prayer:**

Father, heal me today of the "if onlys" and help me to see the potential and talents You have placed in me so that I may serve You until the day You are ready to take me home. Amen

# *Enjoy Life*

I never thought I'd be anxious about a fish, but I was. I came home from one of my recent trips and even though it was late, I thought I'd say hello to "Jabez," my neon blue, fighting Beta fish.

He's about the size of a fat little sardine, only very beautiful. But Jabez would not wake up. He has taught me a lot about adjusting to life as it is and overcoming loneliness, and I wanted him to wake up like usual.

I have had Jabez over 5 years, about a year before the book, Jabez, was published. I named him Jabez to remind me to pray for God to enlarge my world, which I do every morning when I feed him. But this night, I could not awaken him when I came into the kitchen. Usually I can tap on the large vase with my fingernail and he will awaken and come over to say "hi." He knows if he comes over to see me, I will feed him a few grains of his tasty "Beta Bites." But not this night.

I was exhausted from flying all day from the east coast and I always feel lonely coming into the empty house. I used to have a white, fluffy, affectionate little Bichon Frise who was always at the door to greet me, now I only have Jabez so the thought of his being dead upset me. I was too tired to do anything about it so I turned from the very still Jabez, sadly going to bed.

Maybe he had died from loneliness. Maybe my friends had forgotten to feed him as they promised. So before going to sleep, I thought again of Jabez, so still in his little water world. I don't know if it is okay to pray to

God about a fish or not, but since HE created it, I figured He couldn't get too mad if I prayed and asked for help with one of His creatures.

I remembered how I had loved watching him swim. He was so beautiful and swam so gracefully among the roots of the water plant. I loved watching him dive; catching one of his Beta Bites as it fell from the surface. He would make a little dive with his blue flowing fins waving like an angel's robe.

At times he seems to almost hide among the roots with only his little bottom fins moving ever so slightly as water flows through his gills. I thought of getting another fish to keep him company, so he wouldn't be lonely, but the lady at the pet store assured me I had to let him live alone. I still felt sorry for him.

You can imagine my relief the next morning when I came out and Jabez came swimming over to me from the other side of the roots. I was one happy camper! I was so excited to see him alive and delighted to see me I had to be careful not to over feed him and really kill him!

Although I still worry about Jabez being lonely, he has shown me by his lively actions he's enjoying life in his water world and doesn't need another fish to make him happy.

Besides, if I like watching Jabez, maybe he likes watching me work around the kitchen near his world. He has certainly taught me to see the beauty in even the small pleasures of life. He has also taught me to choose to enjoy my life as it is. In that, we have a lot in common.

Almost 2,000 years ago Paul had learned that too. Even though he was in prison and thankfully, I have never had to go to prison, he wrote in *Philippians 4:11*, *"...for I have learned in whatever state I am, to be content."* May that be so for all of us.

# Whatever He Says...

This has been my summer for weddings...but not mine! When summer was approaching I thought it was going to be a lovely, lazy summer without much to do except lie by the pool and sip lemonade. As usual with one's fantasies, it didn't happen.

First of all my friend, Rhonda Fleming's wedding was in June. She married Darol Carlson, whom we all love. As an actress, she wanted to keep her wedding quiet with only family there. However, she adopted a few of us into the family for the event. It was in a quaint chapel up in the wooded hills above Santa Barbara, CA.

The joy and warmth of both blended families was so precious as Darol's daughters and son welcomed her into their large and loving family. Rhonda's family responded too as they joined to make one large family. Rhonda was particularly beautiful with her famous red hair and elegant crème wedding suit. A lovely surprise for all of us was when the beautiful bride and groom sang a duet, "I Love You Truly," to each other!

Rhonda is still going strong. She was featured this month on the cover of a magazine called, "Wildest Westerns." It was a fabulous article describing some of the 50 films she made as well as her philosophy of life.

Then in July, my friends Geri Allen and John Dotson were married on a party boat on Lake Arrowhead, CA. Both John and Geri's spouses had died and they felt so privileged to find each other and their new love. It was a very romantic wedding out on the lake with other boats circling, hoping for a glimpse of the beautiful bride and handsome groom. At the end of the wedding as they came off the boat, we showered them with red rose petals as they walked between us. It was beautiful to see the rose petals floating down on them and then drifting on the water.

Finally in August, I was invited to be part of the wedding of my dear friend, Gwen Lampman and Patrick Schoonover. They chose the exquisite chapel at the Bellagio Hotel in Las Vegas.

When I heard they were going to be married in Las Vegas, I was surprised. But when I saw Gwen walking down the aisle in her long, beaded wedding gown, amid huge bouquets of hydrangeas and roses tied to the end of each aisle, it was breathtaking. The chapel, filled with candles, flowers and love, was perfect.

The music at the reception was obviously planned with our age in mind, as there was a lot of swing dance music from the 60's. I may not have been the bride but I was asked to dance almost every dance, so as they say, "a good time was had by all!"

This reminds me of the story when Jesus, his disciples and his mother, Mary, were at a wedding of some friends of theirs. The Bible tells that they ran out of wine at the wedding; this was most embarrassing for the bridegroom, a friend of Jesus. When the mother of Jesus heard about it, she told Jesus, expecting Him to jump right in and fix it. But in *John 2: 4*, Jesus says, "*What is that to you and Me?*" Like a mother who wants to help, she just ignores Jesus' statement and says to the servants, verse 5, "*Whatever He says to you, do it.*" And the rest is history; the wine Jesus made from water was better than what they had served earlier.

The thought that is important for us today is the

statement of Jesus' mother. She said, "*Whatever He says to you, do it.*" I have no doubt if we learn to obey the words of Jesus, not only will our weddings go better, but indeed our very lives will be more exciting and fulfilling. We will be more contented and joyful as we follow after Jesus, doing what He says.

**Prayer:**

Lord, thank You today for Your Word. May I obey it always for in Your Word lies the contentment and joy I seek. Amen.

**Personal Thoughts:**

______________________________________________

______________________________________________

______________________________________________

______________________________________________

______________________________________________

______________________________________________

______________________________________________

______________________________________________

______________________________________________

______________________________________________

______________________________________________

______________________________________________

# Bless Israel

Some years ago on one of our numerous trips to Israel, we had a most unusual Jewish guide, Emmanuel. Since we were a small study group of only 16 people, our guide delighted in taking us away from the typical tourist sites. He discovered we had all been numerous times so he felt challenged, I think, to show us new things.

This particular day he said he had something special to show us. I happened to be sitting in the front passenger seat in our four-wheel drive, 20 seat Mercedes bus. Shortly after announcing he had a surprise, we turned off the main highway. We drove down through a gulley and up onto a gravel road, which was just two wheel tracks winding over the barren hillside.

Soon we lost sight of Jerusalem and were surrounded by dry hills with little vegetation. Pulling up on a rise, Emmanuel stopped the bus for us to get out and look around. As we did, he pulled out his little New Testament from his pocket and began to read about Jesus traveling the road from Jericho up to Jerusalem. He paused and solemnly announced, “You are now standing on the very road that Jesus walked on 2,000 years ago. This road, not used now, has been here for thousands of years, long before Jesus even walked on it!”

The thought of walking where Jesus walked, on that very road was breathtaking. Emmanuel passed around bottles of water and we walked around on that hill; some of us walking a bit up the road, sitting on an outcropping of rock or standing and gazing into the distance. But all of us thinking....this is what Jesus saw, when He was on the earth...He saw these very hills...He walked this very road. It made all the shrines back in Jerusalem pale by comparison.

We continued on the road over the winding hills, a road washed out in many areas, so rutted even our four wheel drive bus could barely make it.

Slowly he pulled up to the edge of a steep valley and since I was in front, I was the first to see it. Emmanuel shushed me and told everyone to get out of the bus. We walked to the edge of a cliff where everyone was in awe by what we saw.

Across the deep valley, carved into the cliff about half way down the steep sides, an incredibly large Monastery seemed to hang on what seemed to be thin air! It was precariously perched on the side of the cliff. At the back end of the buildings there was a long narrow yard that had a small area for a vegetable garden. Other than that one little patch, there were no trees or flowers; the yard was barren like the rest of the cliff the Monastery clung to.

Looking far down below, we saw a narrow, winding path leading from the Monastery down to a stream. Emmanuel explained the reason there was only a small garden patch was the monks had to walk down to the river for all of their water; their drinking water, water to wash with and water for the small garden. By the length of the path and the steep incline, it was probable it took a full hour just to traverse the path for their water.

One of the people in our group asked why in the world they would build in such a remote, difficult place. Emmanuel explained that it was chosen exactly because it would be very arduous to attack from the top or from the river and that was why it had survived all these years through the occupation of the Turks, Romans or whomever. It was naturally protected by its location. We were amazed as we saw Monks going about their business, undistracted by the gawking tourists across the steep valley.

We turned around and began the trip back over the rough road, still thinking about what we had seen. As we drove, in front of us, I thought I must be seeing a mirage. But no, there were two soldiers walking along with their rifles slung over their shoulders.

Emmanuel asked if we minded picking them up, that sometimes they were sent out on these hot dusty patrols. It was fine with us.

The relieved smile of the very young soldiers was payment enough. Soon one of them asked if we were Christians. We enthusiastically replied yes. They were delighted as they said they believed Jesus was the Messiah too! Their story enfolded that they often asked for this duty of patrol as they too loved to think of Jesus walking on this road and it gave them many hours to pray for their beloved nation.

They said when we went home to tell everyone in America how much they needed our prayers and how much they all love America because we stand with them in their struggle for their homeland.

Indeed we must do that. We must pray for our President and our country but we must also pray for Israel. God said these people are His chosen people and He had given them this land. He also said, if we bless Israel, He will bless us and I intend to continue to bless Israel so we, in the United States, will be blessed too.

# Roll With The Punches

"Ya gotta learn to roll with the punches!" While it's a phrase we often hear today, it must have been practically a motto of my ancestors with all they had to cope, attempting to homestead in the Dakotas. It is still a good premise to live by.

When things don't go the way we want them to, or the way we expect them to, we need to learn to go with the flow. Not long ago a friend ditched out on his responsibility. It came at a most inconvenient time for all of us. The choice he made was not wise or considerate but what could we do? We chose to cope, to get along as best we could even though we missed his help; we chose to roll with the punches.

Sometimes we have to make that choice in big decisions as well as the little, annoying mosquito bites in life. I was at a party not long ago and a lady was serving pieces of cake. "Jared" who is seven, waited in line for his cake, like the rest of us. But when it came his turn, the piece that landed on his plate was obviously a smaller cut.

For a brief second, Jared looked at his plate and at the other pieces, which loomed even larger from his vantage point. But he nicely said thank you and turned to walk away. He chose to go with the flow even if it meant not getting much cake.

I had, moments before, received my cake as well, a large piece. As I received it, mentally I was lamenting the calories, knowing I would eat all of it, since it was on my plate. So, Jared was the happy recipient of my cake, when I explained I needed a smaller piece.

Sometimes things do work out, like it did for Jared. But sometimes they don't and we just have to cope. Our attitude about our loss, our disappointment or frustration makes all the difference in our life. Our attitude may not make any difference in the outcome, but it will make a difference for everyone around us.

Recently, someone blessed me with a first class ticket to fly to a meeting. I planned to enjoy it, the wider seats and even the food! But when the flight attendant came to ask my preference, chicken or beef, she had to explain they were all out of chicken and I was stuck with the beef, which I seldom eat. At first thought, I wanted to be annoyed. After all, how often do I fly in First Class! Let those other people who fly all the time, eat beef. But I chose to go with the flow and told her the beef would be fine. It could have been worse, she might have run out of food altogether!

My attitude could have ruined the flight, especially for me. I'm glad I chose to roll with the punches.

Joseph in the book of Genesis learned how to roll with the punches. First, he was sold into slavery by his brothers but did such a good job as a slave he was promoted. Later, he was falsely accused of attacking his master's wife, Potiphar, and ended up in prison. Yet, because he chose not to become bitter in his situation, he ended up being in charge of the prison! Finally, God used circumstances not only to get him out of prison, but eventually making Joseph Prime Minister!

I'm thankful my life has not been such a roller-coaster ride as Joseph's, although at times it has seemed to be a rather bumpy road I've traveled.

For all of us, I suspect, there are times life doesn't

turn out the way we want or expect and we end up having to do what we don't feel like doing. We do have a choice. We can complain until everyone around us is miserable or we can roll with the punches and trust God for the outcome. Whichever choice we make, it's contagious, whether negatively or positively.

King David understood that. In *Psalm 34:14* he wrote, *"Depart from evil and do good; seek peace and pursue it."* His version of, "Ya gotta roll with the punches!"

**Prayer:**

Dear Lord, help me to turn the negatives of life into positives....to "roll with the punches." To seek peace and good will with those around me even when life doesn't turn out the way I want. Amen.

**Personal Thoughts:**

________________________________________

________________________________________

________________________________________

________________________________________

________________________________________

________________________________________

________________________________________

________________________________________

# The Auction

The familiar chant of the auctioneer, Bob Penfield, permeated the hot, stuffy air of the huge auction barn. It was obviously summertime in the Dakotas. The "Western Auction" had been advertised as a two-day auction with the first day being Indian Artifacts, farm antiques and guns collected by Ron Quail over his lifetime.

This auction, in Bowman, ND, had been advertised across the United States in antique magazines and papers.

As I looked over the crowd of about 200 people, it was easy to spot the dealers and knowledgeable collectors who had come from everywhere for the auction. They were the ones who didn't care who else was bidding. If they wanted that particular Indian Adze, Thumb Scraper, Arrowhead or Hammer Head, they kept bidding without hesitation until they hit their limit and then quit. The local people (including me), often buying on emotion, sometimes had to stop a moment to decide if they wanted to continue.

The dealers and collectors were drawn by the fact that most of the Indian items in this estate sale of Ron Quail had never been sold in an auction before. He personally collected them over forty years ago along the Missouri River and other Indian campsites, so there was no doubt as to their authenticity. In addition to his collecting, Ron loved reading books about the relics and Indian history.

As I helped display and sort his artifacts, I was

amazed at the rocks and what they were used for. For instance, Hammer Heads had a groove laboriously carved out of the stone so the Indian could tie a leather thong around the rock, sometimes binding it to a handle to be used as a club or simply tied on long leather strips to be swung at an opponent. Ron had found many of these through the years. My fast track education about Indian relics was fun.

But Ron was also a consummate auction buyer, as I suspect many of the people that attend these auctions are. Among the antiques he collected were old horse harnesses, milk cans, cowbells, bull antlers, lanterns, or flat irons. He would also buy strange things (to me anyway) like old school room maps with countries that no longer exist.

There were old tools such as a Stanley Scratcher, wooden levels and planes, a Spoke Saver, a Wooden Slide Viewer (before TV!) and a Coffee Mill with huge cast iron wheels, which turn to grind the coffee.

There was a wooden washing machine that was a delight to the pioneer housewife; all she had to do was push the big lever back and forth which moved the center washer, much like the machines of today, except it was her muscles not electricity that moved the washer. Nevertheless, it was a welcome invention to relieve her from the backbreaking washboard she was used to.

Sitting at the auction, listening to people reminisce about Ron and how much he loved collecting as well as buying and selling at auctions, I agreed with them. Indeed, auctions were a large part of Ron's life, that and his insatiable reading to learn.

Later, while looking in my purse for some lipstick, I felt a small smooth stone a friend had given me some weeks ago. I picked it up and saw the scripture. It fit Ron perfectly. King Solomon wrote in *Proverbs 23:7, "As a man thinks in his heart, so is he."*

It was certainly true for Ron. He spent time learning and thinking about Indian Relics and antiques and in the process became an expert. What do we spend our time thinking about? We too will become, positively or negatively, whatever we give time in our mind to think about.

**Prayer:**

Father God, help me to spend my time thinking and learning about what You have to say in Your Word. Truly, may I study to show myself approved unto God as You have admonished me in the Bible. May I meditate on the positive and pure things You have written for my good. Amen

**Personal Thoughts:**

______________________________________________

______________________________________________

______________________________________________

______________________________________________

______________________________________________

______________________________________________

______________________________________________

______________________________________________

______________________________________________

______________________________________________

# The Pie Social

Still thinking about auctions and how much they were a part of my childhood with my grandfather owning the Lemmon Livestock Sales Barn and my Dad and brother Bob, being auctioneers.

However, as I left South Dakota before I was twenty, auctions and that way of life have been far removed from my thought processes. So it was with great interest that I helped organize Ron Quail's estate auction, meeting new people and renewing childhood acquaintances.

I had the opportunity to meet some of the collectors that came for the Indian Artifacts. From "Toby" I learned how to possibly determine if an arrowhead was really old or made a few years ago by someone without much else to do on these cold Dakota winter nights. Toby told me some of these new arrowheads have made their way into stores carrying Indian paraphernalia, sold to not so savvy tourists.

From "Mason," an Indian artifact collector who is also Senior Editor of a newspaper in Wyoming, he showed me a long, narrow, white broken rock lying in a box of rocks. It had obviously been carved but the tip of the "knife" had been broken and so it was just a broken piece of rock to me. From him, I heard the history of various tools and why they were made one way, in one tribe, and not another. Fascinating.

The auction has its history back in the pioneer days when it was a social event as well as a way to sell things you don't need.

During the pioneer days, often these auctions would be combined with a "Pie Social" where the young men in the community would bid at auction for a pie, hoping to get the pie of the young woman they were interested in. The owner of a specific pie was supposed to be kept a secret, but sometimes helpful mothers would let the young man know how her daughter's pie box was decorated. That is, if she liked the young man and felt he might be suitable for her daughter!

Such was the event during which my grandfather, B.L. Penfield, who came to Lemmon, South Dakota in 1907, met his future bride, Gertrude Moon, back in Iowa. As a child, I never got tired hearing the story of "The Pie Social" Grandma often told me, sitting out on her front porch.

My grandmother had fiery red hair when she was young and at the pie social both my grandfather and his brother, Glen, had found out which box her pie was in so they were bidding against each other! My grandfather won the bid and the privilege of eating the pie with my grandmother, eventually marrying her and bringing her to the Dakotas.

Auctions and pie socials may seem like such unimportant occasions, but so often it is seemingly trivial events that change the course of our lives, forever. The Apostle James, wrote about the importance of small events when he said in James 3:4, *"Likewise look at the ships; though they are so great and are driven by rough winds, they are steered by a very small rudder…."* So too our lives are often altered by insignificant events.

**Prayer:** Faithful and True, Heavenly Father, how I worship You. Truly You are worthy of my praise. I come before You with thanksgiving for the seemingly trivial events which can change my life forever. Amen

# God Bless America

Fabulous events often happen in my life with a simple, unexpected phone call. Such were the circumstances when my grandson, Jim, who is a new Marine, called from Camp Pendleton, CA.

"Grandma, they are having a huge air show next weekend, why don't you come down?" Since my weekends are usually quite flexible, to be honest, often boring, I was delighted to take him up on the offer. But I was unprepared for the majesty and open American pride I encountered from the thousands of people attending.

I often rant and rave at the liberal TV reporters, so to experience, first hand, the joyous pride in America and our handsome young men committed to preserving our heritage, was very emotional for me.

Brigadier General Jon A. Gallinetti opened the air show saying, "It is our distinct pleasure to welcome you to Marine Corps Air Station Miramar, the Marine Corps' premier air station, home to the 3rd Marine Aircraft Wing and the largest military air show in the world."

This year's theme, "Kitty Hawk to Miramar: 100 Years of Flight," honored the first flight of the Wright brothers, all the way to the 3rd Marine Aircraft Wing's success in Operation Iraqi Freedom.

The show went all day Friday and Saturday. Shortly after we arrived on Saturday, the Red Baron Squadron of antique airplanes was doing incredible formation flying feats. Painted red and white, these double winged aircraft made a dazzling display in the afternoon sky as they dived and then climbed, almost stalling out before made a dizzying, rolling dive downward to the ground before swooping upward again, all in tight formation. Often they left trails of vapor in the sky making hearts, looking like they were going to crash into each other as they crossed at the bottom point of the heart.

But then night came and with it the astonishing "pass-by" of the F-14 Tomcat with it's Afterburners blazing and roaring. It became obvious why they offered earplugs. Other dramatic flyovers came in rapid succession. The KC-130 plane called The Hercules flew over, dropping 300 flares in precision, lighting up the sky. The Hercules is a big, fat plane, very useful for the Marines. There have been over 2,000 built in the last 50 years and they are still coming off the assembly line.

Soon the F-16 Hornets were blazing across the dark sky. These are the planes that the Blue Angels fly and had demonstrated their skills earlier in the afternoon. But the night flight of the Hornet was equally impressive with all four engines, 22,000 lbs. of thrust from each engine, bursting across the field in a low level flight in front of the grandstand. The deafening booms could be felt in our feet

The air show continued often with musical accompaniment. Songs such as "I'm Proud to be an American," prompted Marines with their lovely wives to dance spontaneously in the aisles. One tow-headed little girl laughed as she "danced" on her Daddy's shoulders, as he twirled around and around to the music. Gratefulness and pride in America and in our Marines was evident everywhere.

The brilliant, dazzling fireworks that went on for over 30 minutes accompanied with patriotic music was fantastic. Fireworks in red, white and blue, ended an amazing display with more than 30 explosions in the sky at one time, showering the darkened sky with sparkling towers, flowers and drifting snow, lighting up all our faces.

The grand finale, the Fire Wall they had been talking about all evening did not disappoint us. From simulating bombing runs to the great Fire Wall, the Marines did provide, as they promised, "explosive entertainment." In 2000, the Marines made the Guinness Book of Records with their Fire Wall over 2500 feet long. We could even feel the heat from the fire in the grandstands, prompting a spontaneous, standing, cheering ovation from the vast crowd.

There was so much more that happened. But the show can perhaps best be described by the words we all joined in to sing, "God Bless America, land that I love. Stand beside her, and guide her through the night with the light from above."

**Prayer:**

Dear Lord, I thank You for the freedom of worshipping in this grand country called America. Thank You for the many men and women who have given their lives so I may enjoy this freedom. I ask You to watch over the thousands of young men and women who are currently committing their time and indeed their lives, to defend our nation. I pray Your protection for each and every one of them, draw them close to You. Yes, may You continue to bless America. Amen

**Personal Thoughts:**

___________________________________________

___________________________________________

___________________________________________

___________________________________________

___________________________________________

# Self Perceptions

Growing up in the Dakotas, I formed a dislike for grasshoppers. To me they are ugly, scary and jump too much. Perhaps that is why this verse jumped out at me. *"We seemed like grasshoppers in our own eyes, and we looked the same to them." Numbers 13:33.*

It's amazing, when we grow up in a certain place WE deem to be somewhat defective or backward, we take on a certain apologetics for having been born there. I remember one man saying to me; it's great to say I'm FROM South Dakota! Now, for those of you who have chosen to stay there, don't get mad at me, I didn't say it.

But some years ago, I realized if, like the ten spies, I chose to feel like a grasshopper; people would see me that way. Besides being ugly, scary and jumping too much, what attributes would people see in me? I think the main thing I realized was if I felt like a grasshopper and had no value, people would perceive me in that way.

How do we act if we think we don't have value? We don't look people in the eye, we shy away from new experiences and new people, we think they wouldn't be interested in us anyway so why bother. I could go on and on, but if you feel like a grasshopper, you have your own litany of inadequacies.

Through the experience of the Israelite spies, God is teaching me I have a choice. I can be a grasshopper or a giant killer. It is my decision. The grasshopper complex fears God does not will our good. On the other hand, as giant killers, we will count on the *One who is in us to be greater than the one who is in the world (1 John 4:4).*

*Grasshoppers dwell on their circumstances.*
*Giant killers dwell on the solutions.*
Grasshoppers dwell on their deficiencies.
*Giant killers dwell on God's provisions.*
*Grasshoppers dwell on their aches and pains.*
*Giant killers dwell on God's healing power.*
*Grasshoppers dwell on difficulties with people.*
*Giant killers dwell on restoring relationships.*

God will help us turn into giant killers. Not only is the problem in our hearts and minds, so is the solution! Ask God to show you how much He loves you and is concerned for your welfare. Ask God to give you the courage to become all He planned for you to be. He will do it, you know.

Then choose to make Philippians 4:8, a part of your thought processes. *"Whatever is true, whatever is noble, whatever is right, whatever is pure, whatever is lovely, whatever is admirable – if anything is excellent or praiseworthy – think about such things."*

**Prayer:**

Wonderful, loving Father how I worship and praise You! As You have pointed out to me in today's scripture, my life is affected by the way I perceive myself. Help me to see myself as You see me. Thank You for Your provision in time of need, for Your grace and power to heal and for Your restoration in my relationships. You, Father God, are the solution to all my needs. Amen

# Grace and Joy

The Thunderbird Country Club in Palm Springs, CA had a fabulous Christmas air about it with the red Poinsettia's on each table, a huge Christmas tree in the corner and greenery festooned everywhere. One would almost think we were in Montana except for the sun shining brightly outside and the roses in bloom.

It was the day of our Christmas luncheon for Christian Celebrity Luncheons, a group I founded in 1986 bringing Christian leaders to speak before our group. This day we were privileged to hear Dr. Lloyd Ogilvie, retired Chaplain of the Senate.

It was a day I had planned for months. Tall, slender and tanned, he strode to the platform. In the rich timber of his voice, tinged with a Scottish accent, he shared the Christmas story. He explained it is because of Christ's birth we can find and indeed, expect to experience real joy.

Later on, he told of watching in horror on television, along with the rest of the nation, the bombing of the World Trade Center. But then, as he looked out of his office window in the Capitol building, suddenly a plume of smoke rose up from the Pentagon, a plane had slammed into it too.

A loud banging on their office door warned them to leave the Capitol building immediately. As Dr. Ogilvie arrived out on the steps of the Capitol building, hundreds of people were just milling around, not knowing just what to do. Without thinking a lot about it, Dr. Ogilvie called out, "Anyone wanting to pray, come over here!" People rushed over. Within minutes, hundreds of people filled the Capitol steps, seeking solace and help through prayer. All party differences were forgotten, church denominations did not matter, everyone just wanted to call out to God for refuge, wisdom and safety for our nation.

Dr. Ogilvie took us back to the definition of the Greek words of grace and joy. "Karis" in Greek means grace and "Kara" in Greek means joy. But in Greek you cannot separate the two words, they must stay together. KarisKara is the outward expression of God's deep, abiding love for us. When we experience God's deep, unqualified, unlimited grace for us, we will also have joy!

He said, "God is taking each one of us by the shoulders, saying I love you, there is nothing you can do that will make Me stop loving you. I can't imagine spending eternity without you." As he spoke God's words to us, he reminded us that God says to each one of us that He loves us just the way we are.

He continued saying, "I believe a good deal of our emotional, psychological illness in our time is because we have not experienced this quality of grace in our families and we've not experienced it as we've grown through the years and so we end up with the highly polished surface of success when inside is the emptiness of not knowing we are loved with the grace of God."

Joy is the flag we fly in the ramparts of our hearts when the King is in residence. Just as joy is the ecstasy of heaven, joy is also the evidence of those who have experienced Christ's indwelling Spirit. This joy exists in spite of anything that happens.

Joy is different from happiness. Happiness in its ethology is rooted in what happens. Circumstantial. Situational. So our life goes up and down like a yoyo. Our feelings are affected by what happens around us.

It's interesting how we depend, so much, on the circumstances in our family, needing to have things go right to keep us happy. But they don't most of the time. Life is tough. But the joy God gives us is the quality that exists regardless of what happens, and if we tap into that joy, nothing can dampen it.

King David expressed it so well in *Psalm 16:11, "...In Your presence is fullness of joy; at Your right hand are pleasures evermore."*

**Prayer:**

God, how I worship You and thank You for the blessing of belonging to You. Your love is unconditional and indeed, I will spend all of eternity with You because of Your Son, Jesus Christ, my Savior. Thank You for loving me regardless of the circumstances of this world I live in and for walking with me through my challenges. You are always there faithful and dependable bringing true joy, grace and pleasure to my life. Amen

**Personal Thoughts:**

______________________________________________

______________________________________________

______________________________________________

______________________________________________

______________________________________________

______________________________________________

# Restoration and Refuge

It's hard for me to know when I first had the desire to go to Israel and see it for myself. Since I was a little girl in South Dakota, cutting out the Biblical figures for the flannel graph pictures my Mom would use in teaching the Sunday lesson to the young children, I've known about Israel.

Then somewhere in my early teens a traveling evangelist came to our church with a huge banner stretching clear across the front of the platform with the time-line of the people in the Bible, all through the Old Testament, marching along nonstop in the New Testament and inclusive of the duration of the Crusades and on into our life-time.

Throughout all of this, the land of Israel played a big part everywhere in the history of the Bible. Fortunately, my deceased husband, Morry, loved to go to Israel too, so through the years we joined numerous small groups on tours to Israel.

I LOVE Israel! There is a certain spirit about Israel I haven't experienced in any other country. When we were there, we would be so aware that the whole world watches Israel. It is such a tiny land, yet everyone in the world wants to know what is going on in Israel. I love to read history books about Israel. I love to read novels about Israel So it was not surprising I also loved to study the plants and animals that lived during the time of the Bible. That was how I learned about the little Coney.

The Coney resembles a small brown rabbit, except for his very short fur and tiny round ears. Like the rabbit, he doesn't make any sounds, but scurries from place to place as he looks for food. Solomon described the Coney in *Proverbs 30:26, "Conies are creatures of little power,"* we read in Proverbs, *"Yet they make their home in the crags."*

The shadow of a hawk flying high overhead or the soft step of a coyote brings terror to the heart of the diminutive Coney, living in the rocky hills of Galilee. I think the Lord must love the Coney a lot as he lives out his little life among the same hills that Jesus walked. He runs to the very places, the craggy outcroppings, God has prepared for him for safety.

Sometimes in our fast-paced world, I feel like the Coney - totally defenseless. How thankful the little Coney must be as he does the one thing to protect himself God has put in his instincts. He knows to run into the shadows of the rocky crevices. There he will be safe. To us, looking at the dry, rocky hills the Coney lives in, we might think it would be a difficult life. Yet, for him, it provides the safety he needs.

So it is with me. Sometimes I am harassed and distressed. I may have many demands on my day or I'm disturbed by events over which I have no control. Some days are filled with strain and stress as I struggle to understand the betrayal of a friend or the rejection of another person. It is then I feel the hawks and coyotes of this world closing in on me.

But how thankful I am I can turn from these threats and run to Jesus, my Rock of safety. There I can hide in peace and security. Jesus has never once failed me when I have remembered to seek my refuge in Him

It's important to remember we worship an all-wise and all-sufficient God. He has solutions and provisions for our every need. His plans and aspirations for us far exceed anything we could think or dream. If we will be open to His soft nudging in our lives as He encourages us to run into Him, into those places of safety, He will rescue and protect us.

**Prayer:**

Faithful Father, how good it is to know You are my safe place! I can always find refuge in Your unfailing love. Oh Jesus, thank You for being my security, my Rock of Safety and my peace. You are my wonderful Redeemer and Friend. Help me remember to slow down and turn to You for my restoration and refuge. Remind me to offer encouragement to others, helping them through their tough times and reminding them that Jesus can be their Rock of Safety too. Amen.

**Personal Thoughts:**

_______________________________________________

_______________________________________________

_______________________________________________

_______________________________________________

_______________________________________________

_______________________________________________

_______________________________________________

_______________________________________________

_______________________________________________

# Trash Cans

Now I've seen everything! Well, that is what my Mom used to say when she was astonished at something. Sitting in the Atlanta airport yesterday, I was astonished.

I was sitting in the boarding area next to a young man, Chris Cole, waiting for my flight to Boston. A traveler walked up to the large, black garbage can near us, dropped in something and the garbage can said, "You must push your trash in before the door can close." At first I thought I was imagining it, so I didn't say anything. There is always so much noise in the airport, plus, he didn't stop to see if his trash was in far enough for the trash door to close.

After it happened a couple of more times, I said to Chris, "Do you hear that trash can talking?" Laughing, he agreed it was. He suggested that maybe this was a Candid Camera episode but no one came over to stick a microphone in our incredulous faces and we couldn't see any hidden cameras.

My next thought was that perhaps the talking trash cans were a product of pork barrel spending by our esteemed Senators and Congressmen and women. I've read about that in Cal Thomas' column off and on through the years. Did some Senator have lots of money to spend on the airport and this was the result of too much money?

As we watched, another traveler walked a couple

of steps over to a janitor who had a small carpet cleaner and a plastic bag on rollers. The lady wanted to put the candy wrapper she had in the trash bag the janitor was pushing. The janitor quickly informed the traveler she was only picking up trash from the floor and she should put her trash over in "our" trash can. Was this another ploy to bring on the candid cameras? So the lady dutifully put her trash in and walked away, not even noticing the can was talking to her!

Chris suggested, since it didn't appear to be a Candid Camera stunt, that instead of pork barrel spending, perhaps it was a simple case of bribery. The voice on the tape of the trash can was probably someone's unemployed girl friend. We wondered if she gets paid each time the tape replays her voice like singers do when their song is played. Does ASCAP keep track of this too and send her a half cent for each play time?

Of course, the talking trash can does have other benefits. It keeps a lot of people working. You can't just clean that kind of trash can, only a trained technician can do that and of course when it is upgraded, he or she has to go back to school to be trained in the new technology of trash can repair! Now you can begin to see a few of the many benefits of having a talking trash can.

Chris and I continued our discussion, wondering if indeed technology has complicated our lives, rather than simplified it. Do we really need all the available gadgets? Do we really need to have our palm pilot, cell phone and computer all compatible and able to share information back and forth? Since I don't use a palm pilot, I don't have an opinion.

Are we making our lives more complicated than they need to be? Are we gathering or hoarding too much stuff, causing us to have to work harder just to maintain our "stuff?" I moved lately and I'm very aware of how much stuff I've collected!

A simple example is the battery powered watches we all wear. I HATE having to find someone who will change my watch battery. Depending on how far the store is from my home, it could take up to an hour. Just for a tiny battery. Why don't we all go back to winding watches? That only takes micro seconds a day and we don't have to get in our cars, and use expensive gas to find the store. Much simpler.

Over an over, in the life of Jesus, we see Him calling us to simplicity and to peace. He says, *"Peace I give to you; My peace I give you. I do not give to you as the world gives."* Perhaps that is what we need to do, get rid of the talking trash cans in our own lives and live a simpler life. Then we CAN choose to walk in the peace that Jesus has offered.

**Prayer:**

Heavenly Father, I praise and thank You for who You are. You are the Prince of Peace, the King of Kings and the Lord of Lords. My life is so busy today. I run here and there. Help me instead choose a simple life with the One who created me for fellowship with Him. Lord, today I choose to accept the fellowship and peace which You have offered me. Amen

**Personal Thoughts:**

______________________________

______________________________

______________________________

______________________________

______________________________

# Learn to Soar

*"They that wait upon the Lord shall renew their strength; they shall mount up with wings like eagles; they shall run, and not be weary; and they shall walk, and not faint."* *Isaiah 40:31* KJV

More than twenty years ago, I used to think and meditate on this scripture a lot. It just didn't make sense to me. How can we relate the concept of waiting to eagles? They are models of alertness, speed, strength and hunting skills.

During this time of pondering, I went up on the McDonald Creek in northern Montana in the fall with my sons and families. I was reminded of this scripture and marveled at Isaiah's analogy. Take, for example, the incredible phenomenon which occurs each autumn on the McDonald Creek near the entrance to Glacier Park in Montana. Photographers from all over the world come to record the gathering of the Bald Eagles at the river as the salmon swim upstream to spawn.

At one point on the river, there is an old, two-lane bridge called Apgar Bridge which crosses the river connecting a seldom used gravel road. So we all stand on the bridge, looking down river. At this point in the river, the trees are very dense, radiant in their golden fall foliage. Most of the years we have come to watch the spectacle, cold winds have come often enough to blow off many of the leaves so the hundreds of Bald Eagles are easily seen, perching up in the tree branches.

They are totally oblivious to us. They have only one thing on their mind, the salmon, swimming by the thousands upstream to spawn.

It's awesome to watch the majestic bird swoop down from his lofty perch in a tree, skim the water, clutch a salmon in his talons, and fly over to the riverbank to eat, all in one fluid motion of symmetry.

Back home, the memory of the Bald Eagles stayed in my mind and I still could not reconcile Isaiah's concept that we should be like an eagle, waiting on the Lord. Except for those brief moments sitting in the tree, eagles don't really wait (as we understand it) on much of anything.

So I turned to my concordance for enlightenment on that verse from Isaiah. There, to my surprise, I discovered the definition of *wait* in Hebrew is "to bind together by twisting." Obviously, the word wait has changed in its definition from when the scholars in England were translating the Bible into English from Hebrew and Greek.

Finally, the analogy became clear for me as I meditated on the scripture.

To have the strength of an eagle, I need to wrap my fragile spider web strength around Jesus, who is like a strong steel cable. Can you picture it? A fragile spider strand wound around a big steel cable? It would be obvious what is stronger if alone, but when the spider web strand is wrapped securely around the cable, then it too takes on the strength of the cable and can hold a very heavy object.

Is it really the spider web holding up the thingumajig? No, but because it is wound around the heavy cable, then it too becomes part of the dohickey holding up the thingamabob! Smile, it's good for you! Just thought I'd explain it in words we could all understand.

Therefore, no matter how my circumstances are taxing my limited resources, I can run and not be weary, I can walk and not faint, if I am bound to Him.

Is there a circumstance, a relationship, a doctor's report, a financial problem that has caused you to grow weary trying to solve it? This could be your day to learn to mount up with wings as an eagle and soar above your circumstances. This could be your day to run and not grow weary and to walk and not faint.

Simply take a few moments before you pray one more time about your predicament, and imagine wrapping yourself around Jesus. Just imagine running into His arms and throwing your arms around Him. That's not too much to imagine. If you saw Mel Gibson's movie, The Passion of Christ, you know what He looks like. (smile!).

As you throw your arms around Him, I have no doubt whatsoever, He will gladly envelop you in His strong, welcoming arms and hold you safely close. Truly wrapped in His arms, you will be able to face your life, no matter how difficult it is right now.

After all, that's His promise to us, if we wait (wrap ourselves around Him) we will be able to run through our circumstances with strength, we will be able to walk through our uncertainties and fears and not grow weary in the battle.

I challenge you, join me in becoming like an eagle. Thankfully, God didn't put an age limit on the promise from Isaiah, we're never too old to soar with Him!

That's His promise, it's been reliable for over 4,000 years and we can still depend on it. We will be able to take flight like an eagle, even a Bald Eagle!

# His Creation

Life aboard the cruise ship to Alaska has delightful surprises every day. There are so many new people to meet, dialects to listen to from other countries and small coastal villages along the way. I do love to take a cruise. As a new friend from England said, “Cruising is so civilized, we can even enjoy our afternoon tea!” And indeed it is a “civilized” way to travel, no packing and unpacking, just fun.

However, one night the comedian, “Noodles,” said that he thought the people he saw on board spent most of their time eating to make sure they got their monies worth. Viewing all of the tempting buffets, even at midnight, it’s hard not to spend most of our time eating.

With the beautifully displayed food, ice carvings and spectacular views from the end of the ship where they have a large eating deck, one could conceivably eat your way around Alaska! To help compensate, I avoid the elevators and tramp the stairs from the $4^{th}$ to the $12^{th}$ floors and back again.

My son, Randy and I enjoy staying up late, listening to the music in the various locations. The evening passes quickly after we eat another sumptuous dinner, watch the nightly changing Theatre show, and then on to the music venues spaced throughout the ship. There is music for every age, disco to ball room dancing.

But the morning we were all waiting for finally arrived. I set the alarm to make sure I did not miss the Glacier. We sailed into Hubbard Bay early in the morning to hopefully watch the Hubbard Glacier do some "calving." We were not disappointed. Even though the Weather Channel had indicated we would probably have storms this week, God blessed us with spectacular sunny days for this trip.

The Captain slowly nudged our ship, The Celebrity Mercury, through the field of icebergs, along-side the huge Hubbard Glacier. It appeared we were only maybe a half mile away, but because of the humongous size of the glacier, we were actually a couple of miles from its face. We stood along the rails, sipping our hot coffee, in awe of the vast glacier.

The Marine Research Naturalist, Brent Nixon, who was brought on board to show fabulous videos and give us talks about this incredible state of Alaska, also gave us direction where we were to look, when the next "calving" was going to take place. He was watching the fissures with his binoculars. As we quickly learned, by the time we heard the rifle shot sound; the calving was already taking place.

Brent informed us, the Hubbard Glacier was the height of a 30-32 stories high building. And the many ice-bergs floating all around the ship were often the size of a semi truck even though the part we could see above wa-ter might be only a few feet across.

KaBoom! Another huge chunk split off the glacier. This one was the size of a house and fell in one piece into the water, making a 20-30 foot high wave as it crashed and broke into pieces, making more icebergs.

Watching this incredible drama of nature reminds me of how small and insignificant we really are. Yet, I'm also reminded how loved we are. To think God planned this earth with its incredible variety from the jungles, de-sert and glaciers for us to discover and enjoy at our lei-sure.

King David never saw the glaciers of Alaska as he lived in Israel; but he understood that with all God created for us, if we didn't praise Him our Creator God, then the stones would rise up and do it for us. I would be embarrassed to have the stones and glaciers in Alaska have to praise Him if I didn't, so I will. I am thankful every day for the bountiful land, oceans and heavens He has created for us to enjoy. Thank you, God.

**Prayer:**

Creator God, as I see the seasons in the world You created, I am reminded of the ebb and flow of my life. Each day with You can be another day to worship and adore you. I praise You today for the beauty of all Your creation...the mountains, oceans, deserts, the creatures on the land and in the sea each one with a special purpose. Most of all Father, I thank you for your Son, Jesus. Amen

**Personal Thoughts:**

____________________________________________

____________________________________________

____________________________________________

____________________________________________

____________________________________________

____________________________________________

____________________________________________

____________________________________________

# Heavenly Fruit Vendor

Friends of mine have just returned from a lovely, leisurely cruise down to the Jamaican Islands. I haven't been there for many years but my memories are still very strong and colorful of our time in Ocho Rios. A village that was both slow and native in attitude, yet with exquisite restaurants and resorts. Our resort was on the beach where we could leave our windows open all night and be lulled to sleep by the sound of the surf only a few yards from our door.

One of the lovely themes which timed those leisurely days is related to the approaching steps of the fruit-vender walking barefoot on the tree shaded road. He carried on his shoulders two huge flat baskets hanging from a bamboo pole, balancing rhythmically with his steps. As he walked he used to call as though singing a tune, 'Mango...mango...Missy, wantchee mango?' Then the chef from our hotel kitchen would call to him to come over with his wares; otherwise the man went on his way chanting, 'Mango...mango...mango...,' until his voice faded away leaving the place to silence again.

Have you ever tasted a mango? It's a delight; it has a buttery flesh like the avocado with a huge flat stone. God purposely grows them in hot countries because their delicate flavor must be nurtured by the long hot days.

So too is the Spirit in our hearts enhanced by the climate of our thoughts. Are we too busy to take time to sit with the Bible and let the words of our Lord nurture us? Do we think we are so mature we don't need to read the Bible? After all, we did read it once. No, God is calling us today, to sit with Him.

Therefore, let us pull down our blinds early enough each day to maximize the tranquility of our shady 'temples' so that regardless of the noisy cicadas outdoors, we may hear the Heavenly Fruit-Vender passing by, calling, 'Peace, gentleness, love... Missy, wantchee Abundant Life?'

"Allegorically speaking, is there a better illustration reminding us how similarly the Spirit of God calls to us daily? In the same manner if we call Him in to sit with us awhile, He lets us choose all the fruit we want. But if we don't, He sadly goes His way until the next day or the next, or until we invite Him to enter and sit with us awhile.

*"...Today, if you hear his voice, harden not your hearts...." Hebrews 3:15*

**Prayer:**

Spirit of the Living Lord, You are such a gentleman...never forcing Yourself on anyone...waiting patiently, gently calling me to come sit by Your side. Only You nurture my heart and provide true peace and tranquility. Because of Jesus, I can draw close to You, to sit with You. Help me to abide in You as I read the scriptures while You speak so lovingly and gently to me—drawing me into Your nurturing embrace. Amen.

# Unexplainable Predicaments

It is at daybreak, before the sun gets hot, that I love to walk in the desert close to our home. There is one particular area I can walk where there is a sandy, flat bed between high hills. Just beyond the curve in the small valley, less than a fourth of a mile, there is a large flat rock. It's perfect for sitting on, spreading out my Bible and reading. As I look around, I can't see anything except the high barren, rocky hills and the flat sandy bed between the hills, created by the rain as it sheds down the rocky slopes on its way to the valley floor.

Sometimes I can almost imagine that I am one of the Israelites as I look around at the majestic beauty of the spasmodically growing plants, bushes, and straggly trees that seem to survive in spite of the incredible heat.

One day while walking in the hills, I looked down at my feet and saw a wood chip, bleached white by the desert sun. Being a "connoisseur" of driftwood, I bent down to pick it up.

Underneath was a most astonishing sight! A tiny plant with a miniscule red flower was struggling to grow. But it seemed overwhelmed by the piece of wood.

As I rested there on the rock, I realized, we too may be like the miniature plant, wrestling under our own chunk of wood. Wood that seems to be a source of distress.

My friend Ellen's house just didn't sell - but subsequently she realized God's protection. Had it sold, she planned to move to another state and marry a non-

Christian man. As time went on, she realized the foolishness of her plan and thanked the Lord for the shield of protection her "problem" had given her.

*"And we know that all things work together for good to them that love God, to them who are called according to His purpose." Romans 8:28*

We must learn to welcome each situation in our lives, no matter how difficult, as an opportunity for our faith in God's love and care to be acknowledged. Through illness, broken relationships, financial problems or any one of a myriad of things, when we are willing to proclaim God's goodness in the middle of our problems, we become a visible example for everyone to see, indeed, we will be amazed at the incredible results.

As His divine love and peace moves in and through us to those in our world, our circle of influence will be widened and strengthened. Then we will be living out the commands from Isaiah 35:3 TAB, *"Strengthen the weak hands, and make firm the feeble and tottering knees."*

**Prayer:**

Almighty God, You are a wise, all knowing God. You are omnipotent and omnipresent. Help me to check the seemingly unexplainable predicaments and ask You if there is a protection or provision for me while I am there, weighed down under that piece of wood. When You show me the possible pitfalls, help me to have the courage to be honest with myself and others. Give me the courage to walk in the wisdom You give me, always thankful for Your redemptive power. Amen

# Do We Pendulate?

As I get older, I seem to recall more things from my childhood. Incidents seemingly so insignificant, my brain didn't seem to think it necessary to remember the events earlier. Take for instance, my planting daffodils in grandma's yard when I was a child. How she loved the early daffodils and years later, when I had my own yard in the Bay Area of San Francisco, again, I planted daffodils. This time I planted rows and rows of them by our front driveway so they would greet us upon arriving home.

Merrily swaying daffodils always seem to herald spring for me. Even Shakespeare wrote, "...daffodils that take the winds of March with beauty."

It would seem the long slender stem should snap in the thrust of the March winds, but instead it pendulates in the storm.

Unlike the stems of other flowers, you cannot snap them to break off the flower to put in a bouquet. Strong fibers form an outer core around a soft center. It's the inner structure of the stem that enables the daffodil to be so pliable that when the storm has passed, once again, it stands erect and golden-topped.

Who among us, admiring the first spring flowers, does not desire to face our own stormy days with the same grace and resilience as the daffodils? So often it seems as we get older, we tend to become so set in our own ways and own ideas, we become brittle and break in the winds of adversity. Rather, we must be flexible to survive as does the daffodil.

Like the daffodil, we need to be firmly rooted in the right soil, faith in the Living God. When we take time to be nourished regularly by reading the Bible and kept strong by the indwelling of the Holy Spirit, we too can live each day with grace, radiance, strength and ability from our God. The apostle Paul writes about being rooted and grounded in His love in *Ephesians 3:13, 17-19.*

*"Wherefore I desire that...Christ may dwell in your hearts through faith; that you, being rooted and grounded in love, may be able to comprehend with all the saints what is the width and length and depth and height – to know the love of Christ which passes knowledge, that you may be filled with all the fullness of God."*

Yes, I imagine if we truly live in the depth of understanding that Paul writes we should, indeed, we will pendulate in our storms, like the daffodil.

**Prayer:**

Jehovah Jirah, truly You are my Provider. You provide the indwelling Holy Spirit so I may be rooted and grounded in the richness of Your love. Truly may I comprehend the width, length, depth, and height of Your love. Make me strong like the stem of the daffodil that I might withstand the storms of life depending on Your strength to carry me through with grace. Amen

# Your Shadow

*"People brought the sick into the streets and laid them on beds so that at least Peter's shadow might fall on some of them as he passed by." Acts 5:15 (NIV)*

The shadow that is reported to be the longest in the world stretches more than 200 miles off the Canary Islands. The shadow is cast by "El Piton Peak," a mountain that rises more than 12,000 feet over the Tenerife Islands.

Whether we realize it or not, every person casts a shadow. When we have reached our Senior years, our shadow has touched hundreds or more likely, thousands of people. What is our shadow, besides the soft gray shape that is sometimes evident when we are outside?

We can see from the above scripture that our shadow has both power and influence. Everyone exerts an influence in their own world. It will be a positive or a negative influence. The kind of life we live, the type of service we render, the quality of our relationships and our attitude all determine the power of the shadow we are casting and the nature of the influence we are exerting, whether we are aware of it or not.

If we habitually practice selfishness, our shadow will be a negative short one. If we give ourselves generously for the benefit of others, our shadow will be long and lasting. If our love is Christlike in its scope, Godlike in its depth and childlike in its trust; our positive influence will last throughout eternity.

Henry Ward Beecher, a 19th Century American preacher, often told about the chief influence in his life during his younger years. It was the Godly example of a young hired hand who worked beside him on his father's farm.

Beecher said, "Not once did that young hired hand ever say anything directly to him to persuade him to become a Christian." But in the daily nitty-gritty of hard work and farm life, he had joy and enthusiasm. He was a beautiful example of Christian manhood.

Just as the shadow of Peter had a healing influence for good and for healing the sick, this hired hand had a profound influence in producing one of America's greatest preachers. Every one of us can cast a shadow that will be an influence for good as it falls across people.

Sometimes we feel defeated when we are Seniors and recognize we should have spent more time influencing our children. Maybe we were too busy with a career and didn't spend the time we should have.

Isn't it wonderful to know with the power of God in our lives, as long as we have breath, we can begin again! We can ask God to help us have more peace, joy and love as we reach out to our family members. We must be determined to increase the effectiveness of our shadow, knowing it will stretch for generations to come.

**Prayer:**

Father, today I ask You to help me enjoy more peace, joy and love as I reach out to others around me. Help me to be an effective witness by my love. Help me to approach my remaining years with Your joy and enthusiasm permeating my life, extending my shadow for generations to come. Amen.

# A Seed in the Rock

One of the things Israel has a lot of...is desert! Miles and miles of it. While there on one of our trips, we saw how they have irrigated whole valleys and turned them into beautiful orchards and fields.

It's also amazing to see huge hillsides filled with trees, making a virtual forest. What's amazing about a forest? The fact that not only were the trees all planted, one by one and growing in rocky soil; but every tree has an irrigation line to it. The forests are growing in The Negev Desert, all on an irrigation system!

It's a known fact that the Israelites invented the drip irrigation system. It is that system which conserves water and gets the precious water down to the roots of the trees and plants that has enabled Israel to become the fruit basket for Europe.

We also noticed as we neared Jerusalem the hills became very rocky. In Jerusalem there's some rain, so plants grow without much irrigation. For centuries, the farmers have cleared out the rocks from the soil, resulting in the famous olive gardens and other orchards in the Jerusalem hills. Not wanting to waste anything, they have used the rocks to put low walls around their fields as well as using them to build terraces on some of the steep hillsides which enables the farmers to cultivate even there.

One day while we were walking through some of the many ruins, I looked down and saw a beautiful, little bush with yellow flowers growing out of a granite rock. It was not beside the rock or from under the rock, but out of the middle of it. Perhaps a little bird had dropped a seed into the crevice of the rock where there was a little moisture and dust in the crevice. Soon it started to grow and that tiny seed managed to crack the rock even more as it grew, enabling more rain and dust to come in and nourish it.

That little seed has great power. I imagine if I were to try and break open that granite rock, I would need a sledge hammer or even some kind of electrical power hammer. That little seed, bursting with life was stronger than that granite rock!

The Bible talks about the power of the seed in *Matthew 17:20, it says, "I say to you," (this is Jesus talking), "if you have faith as a mustard seed, you will say to this mountain, 'Move from here to there,' and it will move; and nothing will be impossible for you."*

Jesus is saying the same thing that is true of the little seed in the rock which grew into a bush with yellow flowers, can be the same with our faith. The seed of our faith we sow, is greater than the mountain of our need.

Sometimes we pray and because it didn't happen right away, we think, "Oh, God can't do it." And we allow ourselves to get into negative thinking and unbelief. But we need to remember the little seed didn't crack the granite rock immediately. It cracked the rock slowly, so slowly we would not even notice the rock changing. But the thing to remember is that THE SEED DID IT! IT CRACKED THE ROCK AND THE BUSH GREW!

Many times, as Seniors, we may not notice much change in our lives when we start to believe for something. If our body is having problems and the doctor tells us that we need to take a medicine and maybe we need vitamins to strengthen our blood and our immune system, we may not notice a big change immediately.

But if we will continue, if we will believe, God will help us and heal us. If we will exercise more, take our vitamins and eat more vegetables, little by little, we will become healthier. We just have to remember the power of the seed of faith we can tap into.

Even in our retirement years, we can still produce the lovely Fruit of the Spirit of love, joy and peace through our lives and plant them into the lives of our loved ones. Just think of yourself as that tiny seed in the granite rock. You can do it!

**Prayer:**

All powerful, all knowing God, how I love You! How I worship Your Holy Name! Thank you for Your care through all the years of my life. Heavenly Father, as I age help me to take care of my physical health and more importantly my spiritual health. May Your Spirit of love, joy and peace flow through and be evident to those around me. Amen

**Personal Thoughts:**

________________________________________

________________________________________

________________________________________

________________________________________

________________________________________

________________________________________

________________________________________

# Failure Is Not Fatal

In the next three devotionals we are going to look at three timeless truths. They are:

- FAILURE IS NOT FATAL
- DELAYS ARE NOT DEADLY
- PRESSURES ARE NOT PERMANENT

You might say, that's fine for you to say, but now that I'm a Senior sometimes those statements don't seem to be true.

When we are in the middle of a failure, we sometimes feel that it's going to be fatal....we react that way... we go into depression or anger. And our delays may have every indication they will last forever and seem to be deadly. Then the pressures of our lives certainly appear to be permanent! So let's look at each one of these and see what we can learn.

Thankfully, as Seniors, we're never to old to learn that Bible promises don't have an age limit. Isn't that a relief!

Let's look at the first one. **FAILURE IS NOT FATAL**. Failure can and should be our teacher, not our undertaker. If we can learn to view failure as an event, not who we are, we will be a long way on the road to recovery.

When I found myself with an unwanted divorce in my thirties, I felt like a failure. I was raised in our family to believe that divorce was not acceptable. In my mind it didn't matter that my husband chose other women over me. No, I was the failure. In my despair I thought if I had been smarter, even though I was on the Honor Roll in High School with A's in college, I might not have had a divorce. Or maybe if I was prettier, or funnier or thinner (I was skinny then!), maybe he wouldn't have had to have girl friends.

It was years later when I heard Zig Ziglar say in one of his motivational talks, "failure is an event, not who you are." I didn't know that. Prior to hearing Zig, I viewed my unwanted divorce as who I was, not just an event in my past. I didn't know it was an event I could learn from.

If we choose to view failure as our teacher, it should challenge us to new heights of accomplishment, not pull us down to despair. From honest failure can come valuable experience; from experience, wisdom; from wisdom, implemented in our lives – SUCCESS!

Jesus said in *Luke 8:50 AMP, "Do not be seized with alarm or struck with fear; simply believe."* Inside of you and me is an inner "believer" that is subject to our will. We can use it to believe wrong and produce fear and failure or we can use it to believe what is right and produce faith and success.

Our "believer" is like a lovely belt I bought the other day. I thought it was so clever. One side of it is gold leather and the other side is silver leather. I can wear it with either side showing, according to my will, or my desires. Our emotions of fear and faith (therefore failure and success) are like the belt. We can wear either side out. It's our choice.

Remember, failure is not fatal, unless we choose to let it be.

# Delays Are Not Deadly

This is the second of the three timeless truths we are going to look at today.

- FAILURE IS NOT FATAL
- DELAYS ARE NOT DEADLY
- PRESSURES ARE NOT PERMANENT

Now let's look at the second point – **DELAYS ARE NOT DEADLY**. Too often we equate delay with defeat. By delay I do not mean procrastination. No, it's delays in our answers to prayer. I'm a type A personality, and I'm sure God probably is too; after all, look at all He did in six days. (smile)

Nevertheless, I've come to recognize that delays are often God's way of teaching us patience. And if you're a Senior like I am, you've probably already learned patience is more than a virtue, it's a daily necessity. It's not an elective in the school of life; it's a required course.

Everywhere we go, we need patience. Standing in line at the post office, grocery store or doctor's office sometimes requires an inordinate amount of patience. Remember a few years ago when we had a perceived gas shortage and people became very frustrated in the long lines waiting for gas, sometimes cutting in. Of course the newspapers and TV stations were happy to report the impatience of everyone.

James 1:3 and 4 talks about patience, in fact as

*James* describes it, it's almost humorous, unless you find yourself in that spot right now. He says, *"Dear brother, is your life full of difficulties and temptations? Then be happy, for when the way is rough, your patience has a chance to grow. So let it grow, and don't try to squirm out of your problems. For when your patience is finally in full bloom, then you will be ready for anything, strong in character, full and complete."*

Playing golf has taught me a lot about patience. There are so many opportunities to have to choose to be patient while playing golf. For instance, simply having to wait for the slow foursome ahead of you; why do they have to take so long to line up their put! Of course, everyone knows if you rush your back swing, you'll end up with a poor shot or at best, at least diminished power.

Bobby Clampett was quoted in Golf Illustrated about his own defeat in the 1982 British Open when he went from a 7 stroke lead to tenth-place. He said, "No game has ever required the character trait of patience more than the game of golf. A patient attitude is a never-give-up attitude. Without patience you cannot be a consistent performer; without patience you cannot reach your potential; without patience you cannot win." Obviously, that statement can be applied to every area of our lives.

Perhaps instead of fussing about the delays in our lives, losing patience with the people in our world, perhaps, just perhaps, we should, like James suggested, be happy and not try to squirm out of our problems. Truly, patience will give us strength to persevere when difficulties and problems come into our lives. When we are patient and trust in God, we will see Him bring us through. Indeed, delays are not deadly unless we make them so.

# Pressures Are Not Permanent

Let's look at the Three Timeless Truths again.

- FAILURE IS NOT FATAL
- DELAYS ARE NOT DEADLY
- PRESSURES ARE NOT PERMANENT

Today we're going to look at the last of the three timeless truths, **PRESSURES ARE NOT PERMANENT**. As we look back through the years on our lives, we see evidence that indeed, pressures, problems and stress change and go with the ebb of life.

Perhaps some of the most comforting words in the Bible are "And it came to pass..." Pressures do not come to stay...they come to pass. There are days we may not believe that some issue, some problem will ever pass, but it will. It will.

Pressures are temporary and transitory like many of the irritations and vexations which we have all experienced. They will be diminished when we realize that our internal resources are much stronger than the external pressures. How do I know that? Well, if you have a relationship with Jesus, John gives us that promise in *1 John 4:4, "...greater is He that is in you than he that is in the world."*

Sometimes I think it would be marvelous if we didn't have any problems, any pressures and could just sail through life, untouched by heartache. But that's not life. However, the Lord Himself has told us how to be triumphant in our predicaments. *John 16:33 KJV says, "These things have I spoken unto you, that in Me ye might have peace. In the world ye shall have tribulation: but be of good cheer (there it is again – be happy!) for I have overcome the world."*

With these words Jesus told his disciples to take courage. In spite of the inevitable struggles they would face, they would not be alone. Jesus does not abandon us, either. If we remember that the ultimate victory has already been won, we can claim the peace of Christ in the most troublesome times.

A good analogy of how Christ has already won the victory is a World War II story I found.

The well known General, George Patton, Jr. was widely acclaimed for his rapid invasion of Germany. After his front line combat units had conquered an area, an army of occupation marched in and quickly took over. Their function was to hold on to what the fighting troops had already attained. Their project was to establish law and order in the region. Those in the army of occupation never actually had to fight the war, because men before them had already done that. They just had to occupy.

So too, Jesus Christ has already conquered sin and death on the cross. He won the battle for us. He secured the provision for us to be victorious in all areas of our life, as HIS army of occupation on the earth today. Paul wrote in *Romans 8:37, "For we are more than conquerors through Him that loved us."*

Indeed, our pressures are not permanent but they are circumstances God uses to build character, tenacity and faith. The result is we will be able to stand and come out victorious through our faith in God. The victory is ours. Jesus won it for us. It is ours today!

# Our Journey

We looked at some concepts in the three previous devotionals, Failure Is Not Fatal, Delays Are Not Deadly and Pressures Are Not Permanent. One contiguous thread that came through all of them is that it is a process, a journey.

It may seem rather obvious to say we are on a journey, but sometimes the obvious is overlooked. As we pass the 50+ mark in our lives, do we take time to evaluate where we have been and where we are going?

One friend of mine told me her retired husband said he had accomplished all he wanted to do in life and now, in his opinion, it was a downhill slide all the way. He went on to say his best days were behind him and he didn't want her to "push" him into anything new. As far as he was concerned, his life, as he had known it, was over.

How sad. Life never has to be "over" as long as we still have breath. There are always new mountains to climb, new things to learn and new activities to attempt if we choose to. Now that we are in our Senior years, however, and whenever we are ready to define that, may I suggest we look even more deeply into our Spiritual Journey during this phase of our lives.

Our life can be a journey of the soul, a journey of the spirit that leads us to new mountaintop experiences in life. Maybe we've been so busy, we've neglected our inner person. This could be the time, to begin to listen to our spirit and to God.

To fully experience the blessings we will encounter along the way, we must prepare for our spiritual journey by spending time in silence with God. Does that sound scary to you? It need not be.

It can be as simple as what I did a few nights ago. I sat out on the patio in the cool summer evening. My little dog, Sir Bentley, was busy chasing leaves in the early twilight. Leisurely, the moon ascended over the mountains. Without uttering a sound, I began to thank God for my life. For His blessings and His care. I gazed at the stars, mountains, trees, flowers and silently sent prayers of praise for each object my eyes rested on.

With no phones, no voices, no radio, no TV to interrupt my synergism with God, I began to notice the soft evening breeze caressing my face and I connected with the wonder of the Almighty God, Jehovah. I let go of my own thoughts and preconceived notions about how things should be and just relished God's Presence there in the gentle evening.

In the silence with God, I sensed what I need to know for this moment, for this phase of my life. I began to comprehend, with a deeper level of trust, that God will lead me to those people and experiences that will bless my spiritual journey, in this, my Senior years. This journey is available to you too.

Thankfully, God's promises don't have an age limit and so, once again we can lay claim to Isaiah 55:12, "*For you shall go out with joy, and be led back in peace; the mountains and the hills shall break forth into singing before you.*"

**Prayer:**

Dear Lord, thank You for loving me and for the beauty of Your creation. As I sit alone with You my heart is overwhelmed that You care so much for me. No matter what age I am, I am valuable to You. Amen.

# Wisdom & Balance

The giant Saguaro (pronounced sa-war-oh) cactus is Arizona's trademark. I remember the first time I drove from Palm Springs to Phoenix. I had heard there was a literal "forest" of Saguaro's along Highway #10, the road to Phoenix. But I wasn't prepared for the myriad of sizes and shapes of the Saguaros. Most of the publicity photos are of very old Saguaros with numerous arms reaching toward the sun.

As I began to study about the incredible Saguaro, I found there were many lessons we can learn from this marvelous creation of God's.

One of the lessons I discovered was the analogy of the unusual growth pattern of this cactus. The center stalk is always straight and only when the stalk (many years later) starts to tilt toward the sun does it develop an "arm" on the opposite side for balance. Then, as it begins leaning that way, it grows an arm on the other side, and so on. Always staying in balance.

Should we not strive for the same balance in our own lives? As we bask in the warmth of the Son's Love, should we not desire to understand the whole counsel of God and therefore stay in balance, functioning in wisdom?

It would be wonderful if I could say I have lived my whole life making wise decisions. Thankfully, I have made more wise decisions than unwise, but the ramifications of the unwise decisions we make tend to live with us for a lifetime.

How do we get our life out of balance? How do we walk in a lack of wisdom? I think any one of us is vulnerable at any given stage of our lives. Just as the Saguaro constantly has to be vigilant to be aware when it is tilting and grow another arm on the other side to balance, so we, too, must be cognizant of the areas in which we are susceptible.

For instance, I love chocolate! Now please, don't anyone reading this devotional book think they are doing me a favor and send me chocolate. I have no willpower when it comes to chocolate.

However, I know where all the best chocolate is made in each region of the world I have traveled. Huckleberry chocolate from Montana; rich dark chocolate from a little shop in the diamond district of Antwerp, Belgium; coffee flavored chocolate from a Mexican lady in a little alley in Tijuana; Macadamia chocolates from Hawaii, and handmade chocolate from a little shop in Bethlehem; my list could continue. Wow, my mouth is watering as I am typing this paragraph, just remembering the rich taste of the various chocolates.

However, if I ate as much as I would like, I would blow up like a balloon. I have no willpower and if I buy a pound of chocolate, I'll eat it. So now I just buy a couple of pieces. It is easier to have willpower when you don't have any in the house!

Eliminating the temptation is my way of living in balance, walking in wisdom. The apostle Paul encouraged us about temptation when he wrote to the Corinthian church in *1Corthinians10:13*, *"No temptation has overtaken you except such as is common to man; but God is faithful, who will not allow you to be tempted beyond what you are able, but with the temptation will also make the way of escape…."*

# *Our* DNA

Wisdom and balance are not the only lessons we can learn from the life of the Saguaro. Georgeann and her husband, Don, sent me some more interesting data about God's unique creation, the Saguaro.

Saguaros are grown in the wild from a tiny seed, attaining sometimes only an inch to seven inches of growth in a year. Often in 75 years it will be less than ten feet tall, and maybe in 150 years it might be as high as 35 feet, although it may live up to 200 years.

Just as God has created plants with unique capabilities to live in the jungle, He had to give the Saguaro some very special qualities. There are often hot, arid winds that blow in the desert. Some of the Saguaro's roots are designed to crawl under the desert floor and wrap themselves around huge boulders under the sand, anchoring the cactus against the high desert winds. How do certain roots know to search for rocks to envelop and other roots go looking for water under the desert? I have no clue, except that God put it in their DNA.

If we are a child of God, we too have a special DNA in our spirit. We are created to learn to anchor ourselves to God during the "desert times" of our lives. When adversity hits and our world experiences an onslaught, we have an Anchor for our soul, Jesus.

Heavy rains also come sometimes in the desert and at these times the Saguaro seems to get "fat." The Saguaro has a kind of accordion structure that expands as it fills up with water, regressing with the spines more sharply defined in the months of drought. Yet, through times of copiousness or aridity, the Saguaro produces a crown of magnificent, fragrant, cream colored flowers every spring.

When the flower dries up and dies, the top becomes even more wondrous as it turns into a deep red fruit which splits into three petal-like sections that attract and provide food for many birds and animals. The Saguaro's ability to bloom and produce fruit is directly related to its incredible capacity to store water, which enables it to withstand severe droughts and still produce the crown of beautiful flowers.

In reality, the Saguaro with its big thorns and weird arms sticking out at all angles is rather ugly. Mankind is also quite ugly when we are living in our sin with our anger, resentment and bitterness consuming us. But oh, when God makes us into a new creation and we begin to develop God-like qualities in our lives, we will be like the Saguaro, with its exquisite, creamy fragrant blossoms and fruit. A shining example of God's love and care for the world to see.

I have no doubt that God desires us to be like the Saguaro in our steadfastness and determination to survive the tempests as well as drought in our lives. But isn't it even more of an honor to the Lord if we not only survive, but produce the Fruit of the Spirit in our lives so people will see the shining beauty of Jesus while we are going through the tough times of our lives?

*Ephesians 2:10, "For we are His workmanship, created in Christ Jesus for good works, which God prepared beforehand that we should walk in them."*

**Prayer:** Father, create in me the qualities of a fruitful life so I may be an example of Your love and care to those in a lost world. Amen

# Uniquely Loved

A Rose is a rose is a rose. Similarly, an elephant is an elephant is an elephant. Well, not exactly.

Elephants have numerous unique characteristics. For example, they make many different sounds. They trumpet, grunt, scream, purr and rumble. Researchers have found they have a different sound to express every emotion.

There are two different kinds of elephants. The elephant from India is about nine feet tall and has small ears. The African elephant is taller, usually about eleven feet tall with large, flapping ears. The tusks of the African elephant tend to curve upward more than the Indian elephant.

However, each and every elephant has his own "fingerprint" on his lower leg. The pattern of creases in the joint just above the foot is different with each elephant. God gave each elephant his own identity through his creases, just like he did us, with our own fingerprints.

David understood uniqueness. In *Psalm 139:14 TLB,* David wrote, *"Thank you for making me so wonderfully complex! It is amazing to think about. Your workmanship is marvelous - and how well I know it."*

As we read in the above Scripture, David comprehended how significant we are to God. Later, the Lord spoke through Jeremiah, *"I have loved you with an everlasting love; I have drawn you with loving kindness." Jeremiah 31:3* He loves us individually because of who we are. Who are we? In ourselves, nothing. But because of belonging to Him we, each one of us, are unique and without equal in His sight.

Sometimes, though, being different can be disturbing. Perhaps we wish we looked more like others or had their personality traits. Our culture glorifies certain characteristics and we strive to attain to that level of perceived perfection.

Instead of being discontented, let's learn to rejoice in our individuality. As we submit our personalities to the working and cleansing of the Holy Spirit, we will become Christ-like, while still retaining the uniqueness God gave us.

In that same chapter of Psalm 139, David, through inspiration, told us that God was there when we were being formed in our mother's womb. Since He was there, He took time to give us specific, distinct attributes so we will be able to worship His majesty and praise Him for being our God.

Let's rejoice in who we are; we are breath-taking to Him.

**Prayer:**

Heavenly Father, I don't mean to be irreverent, for truly You are Jehovah God Almighty. You must have had fun creating the variety of animals and plants you did. Each one is so unique, specifically designed for its environment. But then, You must have really had fun when you made us. We are definitely unique and sometimes even funny looking. Father, I am rejoicing today in who You have created me to be. Thank you for loving me and working in my life. Amen.

# The Wisdom of Man

It has been years since I've been to a Charlie Daniels concert, at least four or five years and then probably ten years before that. Now, I'm not one of those people who can quote a lot of statistics about Charlie. I've always just liked his music.

So, when I saw the ad in the paper, I called to get tickets and invited Elaine, a friend, to go with me. We arrived early and immediately went over to chat with some friends. I was surprised at some of the people I saw there. I didn't know they were country music fans, but then they probably wondered that about me!

While waiting for the concert to begin, I remembered how much I enjoyed him in the movie, Urban Cowboy. He has recorded so many memorable albums, some more country (my preference) than others and some with more of a rock sound.

Charlie began his concert with some of his older, well known songs and then moved into some patriotic songs such as This Ain't No Rag, It's a Flag and America, I Believe in You. Then he spoke about his travels with the USO to entertain the troops in Iraq. He said, "No matter what you hear on TV or elsewhere, we are winning the war in Iraq. And the people love us there!" At that point, people jumped up and clapped and screamed in approval of his statement. It was very heart warming.

But of course, my favorite album of his is, "Songs from the Longleaf Pines," which is a gospel album. I've Found a Hiding Place, Softly and Tenderly and How Great Thou Art are some of the songs on the album. The strength of Charlie's faith comes through loud and clear on this album.

Interestingly, Charlie spoke very clearly about his faith at the concert too, even though it certainly wasn't billed as a Christian concert. But about half way through the concert, he talked about his being raised by a godly father and mother and how his faith has become stronger in these later years. And then he said, "I want to dedicate the next two songs to my Lord and Savior, Jesus Christ." By this time, it was very quiet and everyone was listening to Charlie.

His previous songs had been full of rhythm and volume resulting sometimes in not being able to hear his words. For these two songs, Charlie simply sat on a stool and with very simple, melodic background music, he sang his songs. We could hear, for the first time that night, the beauty and depth of Charlie's voice. He sang, "Simple Man," and his second song, "Heart of My Heart," was especially beautiful. When he finished singing that song, people clapped and screamed and whistled. It was electrifying!

On Charlie's fan website, they said in his bio that his music ranges from bluegrass to country to "straight out of the Bible, God-fearing gospel," which really attests to Charlie's fans. Whether or not they agree with him about his faith, they respect him enough to listen when he talks and when he sings about his "Lord and Savior, Jesus Christ."

After the concert, I admired him even more for the clear defense of his faith in Jesus. Indeed, may all of us be willing to take a stand when we are in situations where we know not everyone will agree with us. Charlie's attitude reminded me of *1 Corinthians 2:5, "that your faith should not be in the wisdom of men but in the power of God."*

# A Senior Moment

The large group of writers, over 200, had all gathered in Santa Fe, New Mexico, to hone their skills and learn about the latest Christian markets open to freelancers.

The camp grounds where the conference is held is in the hills above Santa Fe. It was fall, the beech trees down by the small lake had all turned golden, a lovely sight for me, coming from palm trees and other varieties of trees that don't change with the seasons. Even though it was September, there was a crispness in the air that I found so delightful, driving only the day before from the Palm Springs, CA area of the desert where I live.

At the first morning session, the conference leader gave us our schedules and directions to where the lunches were served.

Then she said, "This next notice is especially for those of you who have come from a lower altitude than we are here. The altitude level here is around 8,000 feet and so if you have come, like some conferees, from a lower altitude level, you need to know that you will probably be out of breath if you walk very much. So, if it is affecting you, take it easy today. By tomorrow you will be more used to the altitude and probably will not get out breath.

But there is one more thing you should be aware of. Due to the thinner air, and therefore less oxygen for your brain, you will probably forget little things such as where you put your notebook or keys. Up here, we don't call it a "Senior Moment," we call it an "Altitude Moment!"

Well, you can imagine the laughter and the applause that erupted! Now, we had a new name for our forgetfulness and it didn't imply we were getting old! What a joy! What delight!

All through that week, whenever one of us would not be able to find something, or forget an appointment, we brushed it off with, "Oh well, it was just an Altitude Moment!" Not only did it provide good humor, but was somehow easier to admit.

So when I returned home, instead of berating myself for not finding my keys, I simply laugh it off and say, "It's only an Altitude Moment." Sometimes I explain myself, more often it's more fun just to make the statement and leave my friends wondering what I meant!

**Prayer:**

Lord, thank You for Your sense of humor in my aging! Help me to grow in my ability to laugh at myself. Teach me to enjoy the foibles of others and especially my own as I laugh with or even weep with those around me during these years of my life. May my Senior Moments truly turn into Altitude Moments as I laugh at myself and move forward. Amen

**Personal Thoughts:**

________________________________________
________________________________________
________________________________________
________________________________________
________________________________________

# Mi Casa, Su Casa

Sometimes I wonder how I can get things so confused, or is it other people who are confused? Well, no matter, the result is the same!

Take for instance the time I was meeting a long time friend, Joel, for a Mexican dinner. We'd talked about where to meet numerous times that week without conclusion. He lives and works in the actual town of Palm Springs and I live in the area we call, "down valley," so we were, each one of us, wanting to accommodate the other.

Toward the end of the week, we settled it. I would meet him at the Las Casuelas restaurant in Palm Springs. It's a busy restaurant and we had not made reservations, so I thought I would get there a little early to get our name on the list for a table. That way, when he arrived from work, the wait wouldn't be so long.

After about a twenty minute wait, they called my name, our table was ready. I told them my friend wasn't there yet but they assured me they would watch for him and if I wanted a table out on the terrace, I needed to take it now. So I did.

The waiter came by and I ordered a glass of tea while waiting. It was already past the time he was to arrive, so I knew it would be soon.

A half hour goes by, and still no Joel. Berating myself for not asking him for his cell phone number, suddenly my cell phone rings.

"Where are you Samantha? Are you alright?" asks an anxious Joel.

"I'm fine, I'm sitting here at the restaurant having a glass of tea waiting for you."

"But I'm here too, and I've been waiting for you." Since that wasn't possible unless they had put Joel at another table, I walked out while still talking, to see the hostess. It's a very large restaurant with numerous rooms so it would be very possible for him to be in some other area of the restaurant and not see him.

"Joel, they said you're not here!"

"I don't know where "here" is for you Samantha, but I'm here at Las Casuelas Nuevas in Rancho Mirage, where are you?" Joel, said, laughing.

"I'm here at Las Casuelas Terraza in Palm Springs, close to where you work!"

"Oh my goodness, we are a mess, aren't we, Samantha! Why don't you come on down here and then you won't have so far to drive home after dinner."

Thankfully, the Lord knows where we are, even if we don't sometimes. Not only does He know "where" we are, but the Lord also knows when we are confused, when we are lonely or anxious. I'm glad HE has my number and can find me.

His assurance of that is spoken by *Isaiah in chapter 46:4, "Even to your old age, I am He, and even to gray hairs I will carry you! I have made and I will bear; even I will carry, and will deliver you."* What a precious promise from our Lord for these years we are in now.

**Prayer:**

Thank You, Father for the assurance in Your Word that You will always love and care for me even into my old age. I love You. Amen

# Ideas, Concepts & Insights

There is a wonderful scripture I have seen fulfilled in my life, over and over and my age doesn't stop the promise. I'm so glad God's promises don't have an age limit placed on them!

It's *Malachi 3:10, "Bring all the tithes into the storehouse, that there may be food in My house, and try Me now in this." Says the Lord of hosts, "If I will not open for you the windows of heaven and pour out for you such blessing that there will not be room enough to receive it."*

Most ministers use this scripture when they're teaching about tithing and it's appropriate, as it establishes, once again, the principle of bringing God's tithe into the storehouse, the church. God is also offering for us to "try Him" if this scripture is not true. He's saying, "go ahead and prove me, to see if this is true."

I've always known about tithing and paid tithes, as my mother believed and practiced tithing her whole life, giving not only to her local church but various missionaries and other ministries as well. But it is in understanding the last part of the verse that has had the most impact on my life.

It's only been in the last twenty years I have begun to understand the last part of *Malachi 3:10*. Like many people, we sometimes miss pivotal opportunities in our lives because we have become accustomed to the status quo. Life is good and that's fine, it's all we can expect.

One day I heard Oral Roberts speak on the last

part of the verse and for the first time I grasped what God was really saying. That little phrase, *"...pour out for you such a blessing there will not be room enough to receive it,"* always puzzled me. I doubted I could ever receive too much money. If I had more, it would simply mean that I would have more to give. I love to give to God's work around the world.

In the teaching, Oral explained that part of God's blessings would be "ideas, concepts and insights," so many we would not be able to receive and process all of the creative ideas God would send our way. This was exciting.

So twenty years ago, I began to ask God to give me more, "ICI...ideas, concepts and insights." And indeed, there have been planted in my mind so many ideas, concepts and insights from God that I'm not able to contain and process them all.

As you pray for ICI, God may give you an idea for an invention, a book, a song or business plan. One idea from God can change your life forever. God is not limited by your education or lack of it. He is not hindered by your nationality or who your parents were. God is a creative God full of variety. This is confirmed in creation.

I firmly believe God's dream for your life is so much bigger and more fulfilling than you can ever imagine. He didn't take time to put talents and gifts inside you before you were born to say, "forget it, you're too old."

Most of us, by the time we have reached that golden age of over fifty-five, have gone through major disappointments of one kind or another. Things in your life may not have turned out as you planned. You may have suffered catastrophic financial, health or relationship setbacks. Thankfully, none of it takes God by surprise and so He is always there to help us. He never runs out of solutions for us.

Especially when you go through disastrous times, it's important to be open to "ICI," creative ideas, concepts and insights. It's during these times God desires to inspire you with creative ideas. No matter your age, God still has a great plan in store for your life. It is affirmed in *Jeremiah 29:11-14*, "*For I know the plans I have for you, says the Lord, plans for good and not for evil, to give you a future and a hope. Then you will call on Me and seek Me and I will listen to you. And you will seek Me and find Me when you search for Me with all of your heart.*"

It's important you do your part; seek God and stay in an attitude of faith, filled with hope at all God wants to do. We must battle to not let predicaments and destructive thoughts defeat us.

God wants to do new things in your life. But you are the only one who can decide today to get out of your little box and begin to pray for ICI. Read *Malachi 3:10*, over and over. Begin to expand your thinking and trust God to open doors no man can shut, that's one of His promises too and again there's no age limit to that promise either.

**Prayer:**

Heavenly Father, thank You for new insight today on Your Word in the book of Malachi. I ask You right now for new and creative ideas, concepts and insights for the good future You have planned for me. I believe You will expand my thinking and I trust you to begin to open doors for me, doors beyond my wildest dreams. Each day I see more and more how much You love me no matter what my age.

# *Holiday Hassles*

It would be wonderful if our Christmas memories were as fabulous as the Norman Rockwell paintings I remember on the Saturday Evening Post covers. I'm really dating myself now, aren't I? I think I was probably two, (smile) when I saw those bright, energetic paintings of Santa in front of the fireplace, placing the packages under the tree. But for me, those paintings probably set up unrealistic expectations of what Christmas should be.

And yes, I do have warm, wonderful Christmas memories from my innocent childhood in South Dakota. Memories of Christmas Eve candle light evening church services, joy, laughter, fresh baked pies and brightly colored gifts permeate my Christmas past. It was only as an adult I discovered Christmas isn't always so carefree.

My friends have laughingly told stories of their family boasters, bad-mouthers and blame-shifters in their family gatherings. One career oriented friend of mine told of her horror when she took her new husband back to introduce him to her family for the first time. Her uncle, who had berated her unmercifully for NOT being married, when he met her husband replied, "So, she finally convinced someone to marry her." And then he laughed uproariously at my friend's discomfort.

Psychologists say that a big problem with the holidays is that they bring together people who sometimes don't like each other very much. They may have long hidden resentments toward another from childhood or destructive communication patterns established in childhood that are difficult to break.

Experts agree that it is often best to just let things go, even walk away from the conversation even though that may take an almost superhuman level of tolerance. But seldom are issues ever resolved and wounds healed in the middle of the rush and confusion of a holiday gathering.

A parent or siblings critical remark, a scowl or even tone of voice can plunge us back to our pimply past and we find ourselves responding accordingly. It's worth remembering that you will be back to your own life soon.

If you find your holidays less than what you had hoped, a large amount of prayer for a peaceful spirit as well as some diligent beforehand planning will help. Such things as playing Christmas carols in the background will help the atmosphere.

And while you must be with your family, take the kids for a walk with the family dog, go for a ride in the car to see the Christmas lights or go into a separate room and make decorations with the kids.

Maybe this should be the year that instead of giving everyone in the world that you know, a gift, perhaps you might want to give to some orphanage or ministry that helps children.

After all, let's remember whose birthday it is anyway, it's the Christ child's birthday.........a birthday party with gifts sent to help poor children would seem more appropriate than the excessive gifts children receive today. Let's ask God to help us give to our family the gifts of peace, joy and love this Christmas. Let's really celebrate HIS birthday!

**Prayer:** Father, help me to be a shining example of Your love this Christmas. And to remember ...the reason for the season! Amen.

# *Walking in Wisdom*

Norman Vincent Peale once wrote, "It seems that wisdom is not easily passed down from one generation to the next and, as a result, each person has to acquire wisdom for himself."

It's a statement that has rumbled around in my mind for some time. I do quite a bit of traveling and speaking to groups of people, usually women, and I hope I am imparting some wisdom from God's Word to them.

Are we imparting the wisdom we have learned to our children or grandchildren? It is appalling to me when I read that most high school students do not even know how to balance a check book let alone know how to pay tithes to the church, save some money and then pay bills from what they make on their summer jobs. Yet, somehow we think they are ready to go out into the world and make a living.

Have we taught them our philosophy about saving money for important things? Are they so used to simply asking for something and expecting to get it that they have no concept about how much it costs to live and support a family?

Have we taught our younger generations about God and how much He loves them?

Have we taught our children or grandchildren the power of positive thinking? I know it is a cliché of Norman Vincent Peale's but it is still a good way to live. There is nothing more frustrating to be around a child that is constantly negative and complaining. Yes, I know children go through the "terrible twos" but some children are still in their terrible twos, wanting their own way, in their fifties and beyond!

A few years ago I saw a TV interview with Jack Lemmon and Walter Matheau. It was to promote their movie, "Grumpy Old Men." They were having so much fun joking with each other and the person doing the interviewing, they didn't talk much about the movie.

During the interview a question was put to the psychologist who was also on the show to discuss our aging population. The interviewer said to the psychologist, "These two, Jack and Walter, obviously enjoy each other and enjoy life. What is it that makes the difference? Some older people I know are very negative and in fact, grumpy! How do <u>we</u> know what we will be when we get older?"

"It's very simple, for most people, whatever they are in their forties; they will just exhibit more of it as they get older. If they are positive and excited about life, usually, they will continue to be that way. If they tend toward being negative, or controlling or unhappy in their forties, these attitudes are usually exaggerated as they get older."

"So," the interviewer asked, "If we are aware of those negative tendencies in ourselves, what do we do?"

"Well, the important thing is to recognize that you are negative and difficult and then begin to change, do new things, get excited about life! It's never too late to change."

That statement reminded me of Dr. Norman Vincent Peale's writings when he wrote, "If a man or woman can open his mind, grasp the concept of an all-loving, all-powerful, all-knowing God and truly believe that God's hand is on his shoulder, and if he will shake hands in an unbreakable clasp with the Lord Jesus Christ, error will flee and joy and success will abide all the days that remain."

There is a simple Bible verse that's so powerful which explains Dr. Peale's concept. The Apostle Paul wrote it when he was in prison. He said, *"In Him we live and move and have our being" Acts 17:28.* We either believe it is true, in Him we have life and have our being – or we don't. It is just that simple. Take it or leave it. But for me, that is the only way to live.

**Prayer:**

Heavenly Father, with You it is never too late to change and get excited about life. Even if I am 90 years old, I can give my life over to You and through the teachings in the Bible begin to renew my life. Amen.

**Personal Thoughts:**

______________________________________________

______________________________________________

______________________________________________

______________________________________________

______________________________________________

______________________________________________

______________________________________________

______________________________________________

# A Paradigm Shift

We were having our usual time of prayer at the beginning of our board meeting for Christian Celebrity Luncheons and after the prayer time, our new board member looked at me and quietly said, "After the meeting, can I see you for a few moments?"

"Of course," I replied.

When we met, I'll call her Sharon, said, "Whenever the minister would announce that he was going to teach on prayer, I would think, 'Oh, brother, another boring sermon.' It seems that so many ministers say a lot of words, read a lot of scripture and drone on and on. But at our board meeting this morning, you all seemed to pray differently, I want to know how to pray like that. I need to learn to pray like that."

And so I explained to Sharon about the times when my life was falling apart and I needed more than a formal prayer. I needed to talk to my Abba Father, my Daddy. I have found that as I talk to my Father, tell Him specifically how thankful I am for all of the wonderful ways He cares for me, there is paradigm shift inside of me. An unexplainable peace comes into my mind and heart as I remind Him and therefore me, of His love and care.

Prayer, communicating with God is good for our soul and for the expansion and strengthening of our faith. If we want to have a relationship with God that's dynamic and nourishing, we have to invest time in it just as we would with any relationship here on earth.

I believe praying affirmatively – believing before we see, that something good is going to happen, is more effective than praying from fear. Jesus Himself taught this principle in Mark 11:24 when He said, "*Therefore I say to you, whatever things you ask when you pray, believe that you have them, and you will have them.*"

Whether you're in a huge whirlwind of disaster right now, or maybe just feel ill at ease, knowing there are problems with your children or grandchildren or problems in your marriage, it doesn't matter what the challenge is. Prayer is the connection we have to God that will release all the resources of heaven to work on our behalf, if we but believe when we pray.

I remember Oswald Chambers wrote in one of his devotionals that when we are obedient to God, He will move the farthest star or smallest grain of sand to assist us, if He needs to.

Then the last part of our prayer life must be to choose to trust. Oh, it's easy to believe God when things are going the way we planned and prayed. But trust goes deeper. When we continue to believe and pray and rejoice in our relationship with God, we really can trust that HE will work things out for our good, whether or not it's the way we planned. That's another promise too, no matter our age or our circumstances. Indeed, God is a good God!

**Prayer:**

Thank You, Lord for I can trust You to work out all things for my good. I may not understand or see how it will work for my good, but I know I can trust You—it will. I rejoice in my relationship with You, good and faithful Father. Amen.

# Divine Destiny

There's so much information available on the Internet. We can find everything from the Constitution of the United States, to the list of all the Kings for the last 2,000 years or the life habits of the bats from South America.

Want to learn about oceans and fish and El Nino? You could check the Internet or call an oceanographer, or call me. I spent about eight hours on a plane sitting next to an oceanographer coming back from Europe. I didn't get much sleep as he said he was having too much fun talking to sleep. Besides, when would I have an opportunity to pick the brain of someone who was not only one of the top people in command at the Valdez Spill in Alaska, but had also been called over to help Red Adair fight the fires in the Gulf War? Sleep could wait!

Want to change your life? Let me tell you something else. I'm not exactly an expert, but at least a well traveled pilgrim on this journey called life. I can tell you this. Your life can change and I just happen to know Someone who can pull it off.

"Do not fear, only believe." As these words of Jesus resonate in our soul, we can find the power and tap into our Source, Jesus, the Savior of the world. In times of crisis or everyday matters; fear, worry, and anxiety have no place in our thoughts or life. We can eliminate those negative attitudes and emotions as we call upon our faith in God.

Some people respond negatively to their problems and circumstances, rather than believing God can bring good out of their adversities. There are things that happen to us we didn't cause. Although I admit, there are times we also participate in causing problems in our lives by the words we speak and the attitudes we have.

I'm not saying God sends the trouble, but I am saying God will use any adversity we face to take us to a new level of trust if we will just do our part and stand strong in our belief that God will bring us through our circumstances.

In his book, "Your Best Life Now," Joel Osteen writes about having a sustaining faith in God. He says, "Sustaining faith is what gets you through those dark nights of the soul when you don't know what to do or where to go and it seems you can't last another day...but because of your faith in God, you do."

I truly believe and have seen it in the lives of many of my friends, as well as experienced it in my own life; if we will handle our difficulties, our trials, in the right way, God will use those same events to catapult us into a new dimension of success. God wants to do new, even unusual things in our lives, at any age, if we will trust Him with our whole heart.

We may feel we are just ordinary and now, as Seniors, what would God want for us. How could God use us now? God is not looking for someone with lots of money or numerous degrees behind their name, although He will use them too, if they are willing to submit to God. But God is looking for is a willing heart, someone who chooses to trust Him and believe in Him, in all their ways. Even at this stage of our lives, God's plan for our lives is so much bigger than we can imagine. I've found it is often as we trust God IN our adversity we are pushed out into our destiny. The divine destiny God has for us, if we will choose to believe and follow Him with our whole heart.

# *God's Timing*

Since my friend, Georgeann, moved to Tucson over a year ago, I've been looking for a secretarial replacement for her, to no avail. I called church secretaries I knew and told them of the opening for ministry. I told every friend of my dilemma, needing someone to help with the computer as well as help with scheduling my speaking trips, and so on.

I had friends across the country praying for a solution, including Georgeann herself! Finally, I went to a couple of personnel agencies and even though one of them sent a young woman who had some limited experience on the computer, she wasn't of much help. A lady in one of the agencies admitted that they have many more jobs than they can fill here in the desert. What to do?

One prayer warrior friend of mine constantly reminded me that perhaps the person God had for me wasn't ready yet. Ready or not, I needed some help! While we were talking and praying, I had the thought to put an ad in the paper. A few days later there were four résumés in my post office box.

In the collection was a résumé from a young woman named Stacey. She had recently come out of the Navy where she worked for the Navy Chaplains. When I read the résumé of her background and training; I immediately called her for an appointment. I also gave her my website so she could find out a little bit about Christian Celebrity Luncheons, the ministry we have here in the desert. This way she would have some idea what her job would entail.

Meeting Stacey was an incredible answer to prayer. I was so aware, after reading her résumé that she had all the skills we needed and even more. As we talked, she said she had gone into our website and found the ministry very interesting.

"Stacey," I said, "it's like God spent four years training you just for us." She smiled her sweet, shy smile and said, "Yes, that's what I told my husband after I looked at your website."

Being in the right place at the right time is an awesome experience. Divine appointments can be in routine or extraordinary settings, but they are, nevertheless, a wonderful example of God's love and care to meet our needs.

I was made aware again, of my friend's statement that perhaps the person God had for me wasn't ready, when I found out that the first weekend Stacey looked for a job, was the weekend I put the ad in the paper!

It reminds me of what King Solomon wrote in Proverbs 3:6, LB, "*In everything you do, put God first, and He will direct you and crown your efforts with success.*"

Just think, if I had accepted the first person that came along, even if they didn't fulfill my needs, I would have missed another lesson in being diligent in my prayers. I certainly would have missed the blessing of God bringing Stacey into my life and realizing that He knows and cares for each one of us, both Stacey and I.

**Prayer:** Thank You God, for Stacey and for teaching me once again, that if I am patient and trust You with ALL of my needs, as You have promised, You will supply all of my needs according to Your riches in glory." Amen.

# Great Hindsight

As a Savvy Senior, I have fully developed my skills at seeing God at work in my life -- in hindsight! I suspect that's true for most of us. We bumble along, hoping we are following after God, hoping we are in His will, hoping the small, mundane, ordinary decisions we make will move us along in the path God has for us. But it's often only in hindsight, at least for me, that I can see what I deemed as an ordinary, unimportant decision, really was part of God's scheme of things for my life.

Take for instance, the decision to attend the CASA Leadership Conference in Irvine, CA last year. I also decided to have a small exhibit booth. I took three titles of my books currently in print and the prepublication information about my newest book, "Savvy Singles Handbook, Navigating the Singles World from 50 and Beyond."

Among the people who stopped at my booth the first day, was a very distinguished looking gentleman. He introduced himself and bought a couple of my devotional books. I remembered him as one of the keynote speakers from the conference.

The next morning he stopped by my booth again and said he and Hazel, his wife had used my devotional, "Shalom Morning," for their morning devotions in their hotel room and it was very refreshing and thought provoking. Out of that seemingly unimportant event, God has framed a wonderful friendship with Dr. Starr, Hazel and me.

Consequently, Dr. Starr invited me to speak at the Life After Fifty-Five Conference, their North of Forty group and Peoples Church all in their hometown, Toronto, Ontario, Canada, the following April. I was delighted to accept.

Through reading my devotional books, Dr. Starr had learned that Seattle was one of my favorite cities in the United States. When he invited me to come and speak at their conference, he said, "Samantha, I think Toronto will become one of your favorite cities too!"

And indeed, it is. As we approached for landing, I was enthralled at the many beautiful, wooded hills and meandering lakes all through the city. Then of course, my first glimpse of Lake Ontario was astounding.

While spending over a week with Dr. and Mrs. Starr, I discovered Toronto is a city of varied cultures, a city of enclaves, a wonderful mosaic of distinctive neighborhoods such as Little Italy, Greektown, The Waterfront, The Harborfront, The Beaches and the Queen Street West for upscale shopping.

One of my favorite districts is the St. Lawrence Market district. It's a great walking area in downtown Toronto. They have done a prodigious job renovating the big warehouses into remarkable condominiums and lofts.

The St. Lawrence Market itself was just incredible with the marvelous sights and superb smells you would associate with a farmers market. Fresh fruits and vegetables lay displayed alongside fragrant fresh baked breads and rolls. Scents of rich coffee and juice commingled with the abundant aroma of the roasted chickens and baked dishes.

A friend of theirs, John, was there, too, and joined us for coffee out on the large balcony of the St. Lawrence Market in the soft May sunshine. It was wonderful to share stories of how God works in our lives as Seniors, growing in His grace. With the encouraging conversation, hot coffee and warm spring sunshine, it just doesn't get any better.

Whether in Toronto, Seattle, London or Palm Springs, we need to be encouragers. When we live our life with passion and enthusiasm, God will open doors of opportunity beyond what we can ask or think. It doesn't matter whether we live in a city, a hamlet or on a farm, God commends us to live with excitement and exuberance. Paul wrote about it in his letter to the *Colossians, chapter 3, verse 23, "Whatsoever you do, do it heartily, as unto the Lord, and not unto man."* "Whatsoever" seems to include just about everything, doesn't it, no matter what city we live in.

There has always been a love affair between myself and cities. I love the energy and synchronism of cities, Toronto is no exception. Yes, I think Jesus liked cities and would have liked Toronto like I do; after all, He was always going to Jerusalem to preach!

**Prayer:**

Lord, especially now that I am a Savvy Senior, help me to have a passion and joy for even the small pleasures of my life. Help me also to appreciate the variety of people You bring my way. Variety is indeed the spice of life and keeps me young.

# Crushed for You

*"Though your sins are like scarlet, they shall be as white as snow; though they are red as crimson, they shall be like wool." Isaiah 1:18*

The primitive insect, Coccus Ilicis or Tolaath in Hebrew, was used in Bible times for obtaining a crimson dye. The dead bodies of these minute creatures were crushed and made into a dye that did not fade from exposure to sunlight or repeated washing. Since most dyes during that period were unreliable, and due to the scarcity of the Tolaath, it was a very expensive dye. Only nobility could afford the fabric.

It is as impossible to bleach a scarlet cloth dyed from the tolaath as it is to remove our modern indelible stains. Yet in Isaiah's language, he says that man's sins – scarlet or indelible as they are – can be washed away by the mercy of the Lord.

Much as the Tolaath worm had to die and be crushed to make the crimson coloring, so Jesus died. He was crucified and His blood was spilled for you. It is still so. Truly, your scarlet sins can become like snow.

My friend, if you have not asked Jesus to wash away your sins, why not do so today? Jesus will not turn you away. *"Everyone who calls on the name of the Lord will be saved" (Romans 10:13).* It does not matter what you have done or how many times you have rejected Him. Jesus used the word "everyone".

If you would like to receive Jesus in your heart today, you will find a prayer below. Pray it with all of your heart and Jesus will come in and cleanse you of your sins.

Dear Father God,

I come to You in the Name of Jesus. You said in the Bible, ***"for whoever calls on the name of the Lord shall be saved."*** *(Romans 10:13)*

So I am calling on Your Name. You also said in *Romans 10:9-10* ***"that if you confess with your mouth the Lord Jesus and believe in your heart that God has raised Him from the dead, you will be saved. For with the heart one believes unto righteousness, with the mouth confession is made unto salvation."***

I do believe You died for my sins, please forgive me and wash me clean.

Thank you Lord for forgiving me now. Thank You for Your promise in *John 10:10 that* ***You came to give me life and indeed more abundantly.*** I receive that life now in Jesus' Name.

Teach me how to read Your Word, teach me how to listen to You, teach me how to be Your friend.

Thank you for loving me.

AMEN

*"The Lord bless you and keep you;*
*the Lord make His face shine upon*
*you and be gracious to you;*
*the Lord turn His face toward you*
*and give you peace." Numbers 6:24-26*

# Samantha's background...

**Samantha's biographical information appears on the back cover.**

**Additionally...**

**Samantha's books include:** *Dining with Desert Celebrities, A Shalom Morning, The Way... As I See It, The Savvy Singles Handbook and her latest, Savvy Senior Sabbaticals.*

**TV & Radio appearances include:** The 700 Club, Living the Life, Back on Course, The Hour of Healing, TBN, Talk of the Desert, Celebration of Life, Larry Bates Talk Show, CAN Radio, Oasis Network, Salem Communications and Dove Nite Line as well as other local and national programs.

**Magazine articles have appeared in:** *The Christian Communicator, Women's Aglow Magazine, Celebration, Haven of Rest, Guideposts, Plus Magazine* & various other periodicals.

**Her nationally published weekly column is titled:**
*"The Way...As I See It"*

# Invite Samantha...

Invite Samantha to enrich your conference, retreat or seminar with powerful presentations customized to your organization's needs. A teaching CD or books available upon request.

**For information about topics and availability**

email: **savvyseniors7@aol.com**

Check her website for further Information and her schedule:

**www.samanthalandy.com**
or
**www.savvysingles.org**

*Samantha Landy Ministries*

PO Box 911701

St. George, UT 84791

www.SamanthaLandy.com

## *More books by Samantha*...<u>Plus a new CD</u>

**• Dining With Desert Celebrities Cookbook**

A 387 page devotional cookbook with pictures and recipes from celebrity guest speakers such as Gavin Mac Leod (the Love Boat Captain), Rhonda Fleming (Actress), Carol Lawrence (Broadway Musical Star), the Lennon Sisters and Stuart Anderson (of Black Angus Restaurants).

**• A Shalom Morning**

Get a cup of tea, curl up in an easy chair and enjoy A Shalom Morning. Samantha's devotionals are pictures of memories sweeping you back in time to your own memories as she also applies a thoughtful lesson for your contemplation. Enjoy!

**• The Way...As I See It**

As in Shalom Morning, this book is a compilation of Samantha's newspaper columns. It is an array of interesting devotionals designed to give you a lift for the day. The common thread and continuing thought throughout the book is— God loves you!

**• The Savvy Singles Handbook**

This is a contemporary, no nonsense, honest and extremely sensitive book that deals with real issues. This book will help you find God's answers to your deepest questions and most urgent concerns. Samantha's ideas point the way to the type of Biblical-based savvy living that can produce happiness, fulfillment and satisfaction.

**• New CD! Midnight Meditations**

Keep it on the CD player by your bed to turn on when you can't go to sleep or if you awaken in the night. The combination of old hymns along with reassuring scriptures soothingly read by Samantha will nurture your soul and enrich your troubled mind as you drift off to sleep in His love and His care.

# *Order a book ... It's a perfect gift!*

Name________________________________________

Street________________________________________

City__________________________________________

State & Zip ___________________________________

Phone________________________________________

Cut Here

**The Savvy Singles Handbook**
# of copies _______@ $12.98 each
(Plus shipping & handling of $3.98 each book) Total_____

**Savvy Senior Sabbaticals**
# of copies _______@ $ 10.98 each
(Plus shipping & handling of $2.98 each book) Total_____

**New CD! Midnight Meditations**
# of copies________@ $10.98 each
Plus shipping & handling of $1.98 each CD) Total_____

**A Shalom Morning**
# of copies_______@ $10.98 each
(Plus shipping & handling of $2.98 each book) Total_____

**The Way...As I See It**
# of copies_______@ $10.98 each
(Plus shipping & handling of $2.98 each book) Total_____

**Dining with Desert Celebrities Cookbook**
# of copies_______@ $15.98 each
(Plus shipping & handling of $5.98 each book) Total_____

**Canadians** write "US Friends" on check.

**California** Residents add 7.75% sales tax

Tax _____

Total Enclosed ________

*Samantha Landy Ministries*

PO Box 911701

St. George, UT 84791

www.SamanthaLandy.com